D1446597

Teaching Students to Work Harder and Enjoy It

Practice Makes Permanent

John Jensen

ROWMAN & LITTLEFIELD EDUCATION
A division of
ROWMAN & LITTLEFIELD PUBLISHERS, INC.
Lanham • New York • Toronto • Plymouth, UK

Published by Rowman & Littlefield Education
A division of Rowman & Littlefield Publishers, Inc.
A wholly owned subsidiary of The Rowman & Littlefield Publishing Group, Inc.
4501 Forbes Boulevard, Suite 200, Lanham, Maryland 20706
http://www.rowmaneducation.com

Estover Road, Plymouth PL6 7PY, United Kingdom

British Library Cataloguing in Publication Information Available

Library of Congress Cataloging-in-Publication Data

Jensen, John, 1935-
Teaching students to work harder and enjoy it : practice makes permanent / John Jensen.
p. cm.
Includes bibliographical references.
ISBN 978-1-61048-732-0 (cloth : alk. paper) -- ISBN 978-1-61048-733-7 (pbk. : alk. paper) -- ISBN
978-1-61048-734-4 (electronic)
1. Teaching--Methodology. 2. Learning, Psychology of. 3. Motivation in education. I. Title.
LB1025.3.J47 2012
371.102--dc23
2011045626

Printed in the United States of America

Praise for *Teaching Students to Work Harder and Enjoy It: Practice Makes Permanent*

"John Jensen has penned a volume that offers a practical path to serving students better. With an admirable focus on the value of practice and the virtue of disciplined effort, he offers advice that educators and parents would do well to heed."

—**Frederick M. Hess**, director of education policy studies at the American Enterprise Institute, Washington, D.C.

"In my opinion, the importance of practice in all aspects of education has been unfairly vilified by many so-called experts in education over the last decade or so. To deny the importance of what these 'experts' call 'drill and kill' in learning any new concept or skill just proves that they are truly not experts at how children or anyone learns. John Jensen captures this important point and gives helpful practical ways to use practice in learning."

—**Marilyn Reed**, educational consultant with the Commonwealth Education Organization, Pittsburgh, Pennsylvania

"Dr. Jensen has an anticipatory view of what education should look like. He sees the weakness of our current education system, and has analyzed it to develop a system that will produce results. He has an ability to assess a variety of students and professionals, and implement his ideas to create a system of best practices. . . . The ideas are simple, and the implementation is not difficult. It will simply take believing in it. And by reading Jensen's series, or simply by speaking with Dr. Jensen or seeing him interact with students, one will easily be convinced that his methods will be successful if implemented correctly."

—**Trevor R. Waagner**, educational consultant for Education, Agriculture and Technology (EAT), a think tank in Chicago, Illinois

"In a day and age when ideas and jobs move across the globe effortlessly, *Teaching Students to Work Harder and Enjoy It: Practice Makes Permanent* provides thoughtful ideas and strategies for students to thrive, and not simply survive, in this hypercompetitive, transformational world."

—**Tom Watkins**, Michigan state superintendent of schools, 2001–2005, and educational consultant

"One of the great struggles in teaching is finding practical ways to solve problems. A great many books have wonderful theoretical ideas, but they do not always translate well to daily practice. Teachers have to then spend a lot of time and energy adopting the suggestions. Mr. Jensen's book, however, has very practical ideas for everything from supporting student talk in the classroom, to motivating students using a scoring system. The powerful suggestions from *Teaching Students to Work Harder and Enjoy It: Practice Makes Permanent* will help teachers in all areas of teaching and learning."

—**Charles Fischer**, teacher and consultant at the Aspen Academy, Littleton, Colorado

"Jensen has done it with *Practice Makes Permanent*—he has given teachers the tools they need to get their students really learning. That means retaining information in long-term memory so it can be recalled weeks, months, even years later. Moreover, he's done it, not in spite of, but capitalizing upon the thing most important to youth—their social relationships."

—**Deanna Nelson**, Ed.D., former school psychologist, Jamestown, New York

"John Jensen has produced an eminently readable book on what it takes to build deep and profound mastery and how to avoid the traps leading to superficiality that pervades so many American institutions, starting with our public schools. His methods to integrate socio-emotional intelligence with cognitive learning will result in a generation of self-starters with the competence, tenacity, and compassion to create the peaceful prosperity toward which we aspire."

—**Barry E. Stern**, senior adviser at the Haberman Educational Foundation, Round Hill, Virginia

"John Jensen understands that we'll never retrieve education from its current doldrums until we think about it from the point of view of the student. Jensen's description of our 'learn and lose' system captures the ridiculous expectations that a fifty-yard dash through a huge landscape of material will somehow teach a subject. Instead, Jensen offers a boatload of practical ideas to help adults help students to build the skills they need to start learning under their own steam."

—**Julia Steiny**, director of Youth Restoration Project, Central Falls, Rhode Island, and columnist for EducationNews.org

Contents

Preface

When I first came upon the ideas I explain here, I compiled them into a booklet titled "Easy Learning" and set about presenting it to staff meetings at Seattle schools. A middle school teacher glanced at the title and huffed to a colleague, "*Nothing* is easy!"

The feeling of struggle occurs often in U.S. education. My experience instead has been that with the methods I propose, students cooperate gladly, their behavior improves, and they feel successful learning hour to hour. Teacher stress drops sharply, and the work feels easy. I had to give up using the word, however, because of the belief among teachers that learning *shouldn't be easy*. "Easy" means students slack off, and "hard" means they learn more.

Honing this blunt-edged distinction, we really want effort on target without struggle, exertion that obtains proportionate results. If students' effort is effective and efficient, it satisfies them.

Education reform generates struggle, I believe, because the means proposed are so indirect, like giving your car an alignment when your lug nuts are loose. It may need alignment, but without tighter lug nuts you'll lose tires and wonder why your alignment didn't work. Major angst typically goes to issues far removed from classroom activity, making initiatives constantly vulnerable to derailing.

Think about it. Absorbing the oxygen are competition for billions of dollars, high-stakes testing, reporting requirements, states' financial squeeze, collective bargaining, the charter school argument, redefining curriculum, teacher quality, school boards' inertia, and local, state, and federal regulations. We can talk about each of those things *while barely referring to students*. And in their spare time, people defend their turf. Even three reforms correlated with better outcomes—teacher salaries, school choice, and decentralization—affect them remotely.[1] Good designs are often neutralized by inhospitable conditions.

The mixed results from indirect causes invite a glance at direct ones. The shorter the distance between an intervention and its results, the simpler it is to identify what works. As results are immediate and obvious, their causes are more readily discerned and decisions about them more confidently agreed on.

What I see in classrooms diverges substantially from optimal learning. The nearly universal instructional model appears often indifferent to students' innate requirements. If this is true, then classroom time is wasted—either completely, so that no learning occurs, or partially, so that it's inefficient.

The "black box" helps define our focus. In designing a complex system, we plot our known actions and results with boxes, diamonds, and arrows pointing here and there, scheduling the forces we control.[2] Some we're uncertain of. Around them we draw a border and say, "We have a problem here." We can locate the problems of education in one of the three pieces of our system. The first is the vast physical and human establishment and all the resources enabling it to run. The third is the results coming from it—for now, competent high school graduates.

The piece between the first and third contains *how* the system runs, the process of instruction generating the outcomes. This niche I refer to as black because we still argue about what's in it even though we assume that good teachers know (but more on that in *Changing Attitudes and Behavior: Practice Makes Permanent*). Its results are so varied that the federal government felt obliged to step in with its No Child Left Behind, Race to the Top, reams of rules, and orders to change.

We know we're capable of better. A sign on the wall of a World War II manufacturing plant holds true: "Any impossible task can be divided into 39 steps, each of which is possible." But as of now we don't know the steps even to get what we achieve now. Much appears idiosyncratic, arising from the skill of good people, but despite their many clues, as a system we're still undecided. We need to clear up the murkiness in the black box.

Our interest is in channeling energy better. Schools doing exceptionally well tend to focus it deliberately so that motivated students work longer and better. Administrators take pride in a design that varies from place to place, but staff and students commit to it. This suggests that your school may benefit from how you direct effort and explain why. In this Practice Makes Permanent series, I suggest including more of an underused factor in your mix.

I propose not just techniques to insert into the existing system but a basis for rethinking it. If the following were true, consider what it would mean: Every moment students carry with them their primary motivations and needs. Certain responses can meet their needs, improve their attitude, deepen their knowledge, and generate satisfaction. In short, *some responses are better than others.* If that makes sense, does it also make sense to find out what they are? And what if some recur, if they fall into a pattern, and if the pattern might equip us with a habitually competent response?

If you're game for such a thought experiment, I want to explain a few responses that do the heavy lifting of learning and attitude change, and how to draw on them easily. Their organizing principle is practice, an activity offering a direct relationship to increased learning. The more students practice, the better they get. *If students learn poorly, I guarantee that they aren't practicing their learning.*

That's the silver bullet. Change the single factor of practice, and they immediately, within the same hour, learn more. Using practice effectively, teachers motivate students, elicit their effort, expand their hourly objectives, and generate permanent learning. The *how* is simple enough for any teacher to apply to any subject with any students K–12.

Mainstream education doesn't think this way. Some practitioners even hold that what we do now is adequate. They read dropout rates, achievement differences for certain demographics, international standings, and other evidence, and still say, "We're doing fine." Others chime in, "We're doing the best we can," implying "so don't bother us." I write for those who think improvement is both possible and urgent.

This won't depend just on finding good teachers. A parallel comes to mind. When I was in high school, a friend and I went deer hunting, taking a small boat and outboard into saltwater lakes drained by strong tidal flows. Entering one, we confronted an outflow *going exactly as fast as the motor could push us.* Running full speed, we were literally fixed in place, and only my friend and I also trading off rowing as fast as we could got us past that point and into the lake. My impression is that teachers often face just such an experience—working as hard as they can but standing still because the system itself counteracts their efforts.

After twenty years of working off and on with classroom programming, I constantly searched for something better. Then, in 1992, unfolding conditions enabled me to recognize the silver bullet. Watching my son play soccer with his friends, I could see how motivated they were despite rain and a muddy field; yet the same boys were uninspired in the classroom.

It struck me that the problem wasn't the boys but the conditions. The motivating factors appeared to be clear directions and rules, developing competence by practice, and reciprocity, teamwork, performance, and scoring. Converted to the classroom, these conditions are easy to use and increase learning at once.

If that appears implausible to you, could we check how you determine that? Because our thinking is narrower than our subjective control of our attention leads us to believe, we don't notice how our very perceptions sustain a problem. All of us find it difficult to grasp a gap in our thinking and notice a possibility that differs from what preoccupies us. *We can't see what we can't see.* We fix our eye on the obvious defined by our life experience, but if we're consumed by aspects of education that at best yield only a trickle of influence, small wonder that our efforts are stalemated.

If you've been in education long, I propose that *it's trained you* to accept assumptions that undermine learning. You may even acknowledge this while momentum carries you on as always. Recall the extension agent who advised a farmer on how to get better crops. The farmer stopped him.

"Shucks, son," he said. "I don't farm now half as good as I know how." Maybe you already know how to step up your game and don't need more ideas. But a priori each of us knows only a microscopic fragment of the whole, while avoiding the corollary that we're perpetually wrong about everything else. Few of us conduct our lives in the shadow of that recognition. What we know fills our world out to its edges. Our tiny sketch of reality plays through our mind as though it were the sum of all.

Then when our assumptions exceed our knowledge, mediocre thinking infects our actions and we devise systems that reward people for carrying out duties absent of value. If we're in substantial error, we don't know it because our current thinking engulfs us and isn't corrected because those around us agree with us.

Some assert that a secure way out can only arise from statistically valid research.[3] While the Education Resources Information Center (ERIC) entries are studded with it, this hasn't resulted in changes needed. Knowledge hasn't been articulated into practice, though expertise can appear anywhere. A single workshop in an educational conference might be transforming, but we've had this access for decades—leading me to expect less from research alone. Practically everything ever said about education is available to us, yet here we are. The Race to the Top was intended to find out what—something entirely unknown till now?

Evidence-based decision making is a worthy aim, but I believe the present need is more like trying to figure out how a puzzle fits together than to certify a particular piece as correct. We're looking for how familiar conditions and human makeup interplay, which involves the sort of thinking that precedes a proposal of marriage, an offer to investors, or a treaty between countries.

About the big issues, statistical certainty is bogus. We rarely can control and compare overarching conditions, and instead undertake lifetime commitments on the basis of theoretical validity—that the thinking makes sense. We use research better to observe and collect evidence realistically, project conditions into the future as best we can, and mobilize our capacity to respond.[4]

If frustrations incline you to judge anyone, let me suggest skipping that for a time. In my view, the true culprits are long dead, and pointing fingers diverts attention from today's effort. Students, for instance, are easy to blame. They may appear not to apply themselves nor to value learning, and their parents give up trying to straighten them out. I observe instead that regardless of what they bring to school, they're motivated or discouraged *instantly* by the conditions they encounter. Those lackadaisical with one teacher work hard for another.

People or conditions you allow to annoy you soak up the attention you need to use differently in order to get the changes you want. Resources may indeed need reconfiguring, but around what? We first need a solid idea from which to rethink other concerns, beginning in the mind of a child.

My primary context isn't the research but the experience you and I share in common with all who have attended a school. I ask you, "Look at this. Think how it moves, how cause and effect are at work"—from the perception of a passing thought to the channeling of student energy *in globo*. I count on you to draw at least on your own sixteen years of early schooling and to recognize in your children and others around you the features I point out.

Here and there I alight on a few studies not yet assimilated into U.S. education, more because their train of thought deserves examining than because they're independently probative. Points made forty years ago I bring up because I've seen them validated, and I refer little to common classroom theories. They've already been exhaustively argued yet necessarily adapt to what I regard as a fundamentally misaligned system.

Like the hang glider that could have been invented centuries ago, the components of great education have been around a long time but have not been adequately applied. In the early 1990s, I consulted at a school led by a committed principal viciously attacked by unbalanced but influential critics who had leverage over the school.

"When I got this job," he told me, "I swore I would bring this school into the 1970s (!) if it killed me, and it almost has!" His purpose remains valid. Perhaps we can bring the U.S. system into what was known forty years ago.

I may view differently the work you yourself do. My object in writing is to grapple with issues we disagree on, so if you notice a challenge in my words, it's intended. Often I tackle thinking that to me maintains the problem. If you hold it, I have to ask you to rethink it, though I do so respectfully because I know what it can cost to teach well. If I paint a picture of something going wrong that doesn't apply to you, please don't take it personally.

As I suggest a global shift through using a few principles differently, you might respond, "It's more complicated than that." It may be, yet we continually seek the step offering a better cost–benefit ratio. You're onstage doing education, I enter stage left brandishing changes to the script, and you get to decide if they improve the performance or not. I share personally in engrained human limitations and can only hope others will correct my flaws and omissions.

The direction I propose is toward *mastering learning with great pleasure.* This is a how-to goal about method. Twin aims—mastery and pleasure—can guide our actions hour by hour, but we have to intend them because they contradict experience and don't occur spontaneously. Students forget much of what they learn and may labor under a neutral, bored, or negative feeling alienating them from school. Simultaneous mastery and pleasure are the exception, especially for the most worrisome populations.

To pursue these goals, I develop an idea that if adequately understood and applied can quickly transform students' experience. In sum, skill in any field—in knowledge as well as social skills and self-management—depends on practice. Each chapter explores an aspect of that idea, and basic notions recur.

I return often to students' affective nature, their social relationships, the necessity of practicing to improve, of performing to demonstrate, and of scoring to confirm. And if I appear to belabor a point, appreciate my position. When I've thrown in everything but the kitchen sink to no avail, stand back because here comes the kitchen sink.

Some of those I write for have a remote hand in education: legislators, school board members, state and district staff, academics, researchers, reporters, parents, and working adults. Speaking for society, they ask for certain things, but their influence is muted because of their distance from classrooms.

Few immerse themselves in how children's minds operate, and most defer to teachers an insightful examination of classroom activity. I hope to make clearer for this group what to ask for and why, and how to tell whether they're getting what they want. Teachers are the primary readers I speak to. For you, my goal is this:

I want to transform your classroom, blow the top off your students' scores and accomplishments, make their parents ecstatic over their progress, get you a nomination for district teacher of the year, have news media show up to document what your students do, and hear you testify before lawmakers about how easy it is to revolutionize learning nearly overnight.

These outcomes are possible, I believe, if you're searching and can absorb ideas from others' experience. This book focuses primarily on the requirements for academic progress. The next in this series is titled *Changing Attitudes and Behavior: Practice Makes Permanent.* The third is *A Compendium of Methods: Practice Makes Permanent,* explaining how to use fifty-four ways to obtain academic and affective outcomes.

John Jensen
September 2011

ONE

First, Practice: The Nature and Importance of Practice

A SINGLE HUMONGOUS MISTAKE

Most of the ills that plague U.S. education can be traced to a single humongous mistake. Standard instruction violates a learning principle drawn upon correctly in every other sector of society. Schools that apply it even haphazardly produce better results, and those that ignore it produce worse results. If you're in business, sports, a profession, or the arts, you won't be surprised, but if you're a classroom teacher, brace yourself. If you're puzzled, chances are the physical education teachers at your school know it well, so people nearby can explain it to you. The principle violated nearly everywhere in schools is *Practice Makes Permanent*.

Okay, you've heard it before. Odds are, though, that it's been a long time since you thought about how to employ it better in your classroom. If you're an administrator, you may *never* have inquired of a teacher how he or she uses it, and if you're an education money-handler, I'd give you long odds that you've never considered it as you allot resources. That the principle has been ignored is unfortunate, but because it's so simple and powerful it's also promising. It's easy to put to work, and effects show up the same day you start.

What do we mean by practice?

TWO NOTES

In dictionary definitions, two notes recur. One is *repetition*. Actions are done over and over. The other is *developing and retaining a skill*. A law practice speaks to the discipline of mastering a field of knowledge. Im-

1

mersing oneself in a set of ideas makes one practiced at them. We see this demonstrated in the ferocious practice habits of athletes, artists, and musicians.

Seated beside me in an audience was a middle-aged man who told me he was a professional journeyman musician. He had practiced the guitar four hours a day *for thirty years.* In any field, those at the top by and large weave their life pattern around constant practice to develop and maintain a skill.

How to apply this to classrooms is not instantly obvious. A teacher might regard practice as relevant only for the gymnasium or sports field and might believe that no classroom activity compares to basketball shots or football passes.

Understanding the venue solves the problem. Where skiing has a ski slope, repeated effort for knowledge has its own arena: the mind of a child. The action there is the effort of focused thought. From recurrent effort around a theme one develops competence with the theme. After practice has shaped up a set of thoughts, a teacher's question represents *game on!* A unit test given is like the Saturday football game for which the team practices all week, repeating the skills up to their moment of demonstration. Tests and questions reveal the results of the practice of knowledge.

Since it occurs invisibly, managing this practice can pose a challenge. We need to apply to it the elements basic to all practice: First, input: Our mind absorbs a model of the activity to be practiced. Then, output: We run and rerun outwardly the input we received. An idea enters and we configure outer effort around it.

With children, the input–output cycle is active well ahead of the intent to improve. No sooner do they see a peer do anything at all than they say, "Let me try too." A younger brother follows an older jumping across a ditch. His brother jumping is the plan for the younger one doing it.

In sports, the input is the physical actions the coach explains, and output is doing them. In music, the input is the musical score and the output is playing the notes. In public speaking, input is developing the ideas, and output is saying them to someone. Practicing learning has much in common with public speaking. We think through how ideas are linked together and present them coherently—input and output.

LEADING EDGE

These two basic actions make practice possible, but they must be on target. Effort isn't just repeated but is done so that the leading edge of skill grows from it. As people locate this edge and practice diligently at it, even average ability can evolve into superior skill. Children's instinct aligns with this cycle. They enjoy effort that pushes their boundaries in directions their culture values.

Higher, faster, stronger characterize not just the Olympics but human nature. In his TV series *The Ascent of Man,* Jacob Bronowski declared that the main civilizing influence is "man's pleasure in doing what he does well, and having done it well, to do it even better."[5] Climbing a mountain because it's there, or going to the moon, or accomplishing any of the 3,437 Guinness world records are not aberrations of human experience but its natural expression.

Once we decide school time is valuable, it makes sense to find the most efficient way to use it. Some ways work better than others. Even about our own efforts we know how easy it is to practice aimlessly or with focus, on or off target, forgetting something immediately or saving and improving it. Often we need someone else already expert in our skill to guide our effort. The ways to waste time have no limit, and perhaps only a few really move us ahead.

My goal for your class presumes that once you design students' effort effectively, they can learn so fast that even they are startled. But if you don't determine to be on target, you can look forward to more wasted time, wasted emotion, and masses of knowledge quickly learned and forgotten.

INPUT VERSUS ASSIMILATION TIME

A critical correlation helps us plan our time. It's a standard feature of our mental apparatus that instruction endemically ignores: Whatever time we use in *receiving* a new idea, we need many multiples of it to *assimilate* the idea. The input of a single new idea may require four or five times as much output to make it usable by discussing it, explaining it, summarizing it, organizing it, writing it, and answering questions with it.

Assimilative activity links the new idea to what else we know. Talking it out, even explaining the same thing to several people at different times, opens novel connections. Receiving it, we encode it into certain niches in our knowledge bank so we can decode it back into words when asked. Replicability of knowledge (output) validly displays the effectiveness of learning (input). Visible action shows mastery of the invisible.

To apply this, check your teaching methods for how you conduct input and output. Input gets the idea across so students have it accurately, preferably with a written summary they can return to. Then examine their output of it. How do they outwardly express, reveal, apply, demonstrate, explain, or act on the input they received, and how much time do they spend at this? If precision interests you, bring a stopwatch to class and put objective numbers to these activities.

SUMMARY

1. "Practice makes permanent" has been underused in U.S. education.
2. Practice is repeating a model of a skill or idea in order to master it.
3. The effort in the mind of a child is the input of the model, then output or practice of it.
4. We need a larger proportion of the available time spent in output/ practice than on input of the model.

TWO

Accumulate Knowledge: U.S. Education Subverts Mastered Knowledge

Practice is comprised of clear input and repeated output, but to what purpose? Where are we going with it?

Typical input–output cycles in schools today contain a recurring flaw. The very concept of practice means getting better at something, but to get better you at least retain what you could do before. It's pointless to practice what you will shortly dismiss. Why go to all the work if the end is the same as if you didn't do it at all?

Schools err habitually, I believe, in their failure to make learning permanent piece by piece. They choose only to qualify a given piece as passing a momentary checkpoint. Students realize that it doesn't matter how much they actually know later because the system takes account only of their relation to the checkpoint, leaving them little incentive to pursue permanent retention. Too many teachers are content with having survived the school year and punt down the field students' actual mastery of what they study.

LEARN AND LOSE

The prevailing system is "learn and lose." Note how each of its features logically, through students' eyes, can affect their effort toward permanent retention of knowledge:

1. *Courses begin and end by plan.* "Whew! I'm safe to forget this now."

2. *No expressed intent to learn a body of knowledge.* "If I just get the assignments in, I'll be okay. Thank heaven I don't have to explain it."

3. *No complete hard copy kept permanently.* "I got interested in the text, but they take it away from you anyway. And these scattered papers of mine—I can't get much from them so I might as well throw them away too."

4. *Teaching of small pieces not integrated.* "I didn't really get why this piece is here, and they jumped to something different. Oh well."

5. *Recognition-based tests.* "I love sentence completions and matching columns. You can usually figure out what goes with what, and as long as they set up the problems on the test for us, I can mostly work my way through them."

6. *Personal interest usually irrelevant.* "When I was smaller, I liked lots of science things—rocks and birds and stuff. But now everything is just so much *work.*"

7. *Pretest reviews designed to improve scores.* "Good thing we had that review and sample test, or I'd have flunked. I'm glad they narrow it down for the test."

8. *Scheduled tests encourage cramming.* "Mom, our test is Monday and my friends are coming over. We're going to study all weekend. Could you buy us a big pizza?"

9. *"Final" exam declares an end point to effort.* "Hey, are we done or are we done! Good-bye physics!"

10. *Learning and nonlearning dismissed equally.* "The teacher said I got that whole section wrong, that I didn't understand some basic thing. Oh well. We're done with it anyway and I at least got a C– for my report card."

This picture should be jarring because, while one or two factors might occur in an otherwise sound system, *ten factors together imply conscious choice* to produce superficial learning. If you are an administrator and tolerate this in your school, look in the mirror: *You design students' experience to produce minimal instead of masterful learning,* characterized accurately by many students' thought, "Why bother?"

APPREHENDING AND SAVING

Knowledge, we might agree, isn't just assignments. It encompasses one's entire internal model of the world painted in pictures, words, visceral feelings, vague impressions, explicit ideas, and actions. It links us with our surroundings and assigns meaning to the stimuli pouring upon us. While we may debate what to teach, there's general agreement on the minimums needed to function in society and that lacking them is a disadvantage.

Our society depends heavily on numbers and words, a focus that in another society might be on plants and animals. What the numbers and words *say* is a further issue, but first we need to know that we can absorb *whatever* they have to offer us. We're first omnivorous, learning everything we lay hands on, and then decide which niches to claim for our own.

Once we have identified knowledge worth pursuing, attention turns then to installing it—apprehending and saving. The first occurs through presentation by teacher, book, student search, experience, or other means. What distinguishes mastery from apprehending is *saving it.* Failing to distinguish between these two activities wastes time, money, and effort.

Apprehending occurs on the surface, and saving is deeper—a difference easy to grasp. Here's *deep*: A month after a course ends, someone asks you a question about it and you can explain it thoroughly, drawing from thinking as fresh a month later as at the time of the final exam. Here's *surface*: You answer, "Yes, we had something about that. The text was thick. It was . . . was . . . *hard!*"

Two steps start us toward depth. First, we *intend* to save learning and then we *identify* what to save. If we intend but don't identify, activities are vaguely focused. If we identify but don't intend, activities are never undertaken. We register a firm first impression of a chunk worth saving but not too much at once, then encode it in the brain in several ways, and then recall it at increasing intervals of time.

As related pieces of knowledge arrive, we integrate them. We revisit the expanding field periodically until it registers as permanent. The system is the same for kindergartners and graduates: Get a point, save it, get another, put the two into a meaningful field, save both, get another, integrate and save all three, and so on.

Typical learning, aside from core information immediately and constantly reused, instead is to get a point, forget some of it, get another, and forget some of it—resulting not only in education poor in outcomes but also discouraging to students who realize that their effort doesn't finally accomplish what they want. Even their good grades don't mean they can replicate and use what they labored to learn.

Missing from the U.S. system is the "save it" step. We reduce students' investment in learning when they realize that we require them *to appear* to learn regardless of whether they actually do. They comply, they listen, they try to do the assignments, but in their hearts they know how marginal is their knowledge.

To undertake practice, you first aim to sustain a body of knowledge, to continue knowing what you knew before and add to it. This replaces the "bathtub model" where knowledge pours in through a faucet above and out through a drain below at the same rate. Water doesn't stay in the tub. Instead of the bathtub model, some prefer the "wheelbarrow model": Load up learning, move it, dump it, and go back for another load.

PROGRESSIVE EDUCATION

To understand the lunacy in these common models, we look back decades ago when mastery of knowledge was still important and a profound change occurred that bedevils education today. Before 1900, eighth graders often knew more about the world than do college students now. Educators believed that knowing was important, that classroom activity caused it, and that parents might be little help because they were even less educated than their children. They knew what they wanted and used classroom time to achieve it.

Complaints arose that the curriculum was outdated, preordained, and imposed by authoritarian methods. Educators instead wanted students to show up well in the world with good habits, good health, and social responsibility, and expected that guiding their behavior would equip them better than would knowledge. Such sensible-sounding ideas appealed to many, and progressive education took hold, with John Dewey its spokesman. In an influential 1916 book, Dewey discounted academic learning:

> The development within the young of the attitudes and dispositions necessary to the continuous and progressive life of a society cannot take place by direct conveyance of beliefs, emotions, and knowledge. It takes place through the intermediary of the environment. . . . The deeper and more intimate educative formation of disposition comes, without conscious intent, as the young gradually partake of the activities of the various groups to which they may belong.

He builds on the impact of group norms by advocating communication, training, fostering, nurturing, cultivating, setting up conditions, direction, control, and especially guidance, declaring, "We never educate directly but indirectly by means of the environment."[6]

Such assumptions dismiss conscious self-management. But students, moment by moment, don't respond just automatically, helpless to function beyond the guiding stimuli. They weigh their current perceptions against what they know about the situation. While all of us quickly assign routine deeds to unconscious patterning, for anything we wish to change and for any challenge we must cope with, we first make it conscious and then focus on it intently.

By opposing the "piling up of knowledge," Dewey ignored the connection between what students know and how they act. The two don't occupy separate spheres. In any given field and in all the competencies students need, the less you know, the less versatile your behavior is likely to be. *Mastered* knowledge gives people options for what to do. Although individual teachers and schools may buck the trend, schools today inherit a system that rejected the deliberate mastery of learning. Rationalizations for this emphasis have been woven into pedagogy ever since.

COMMITMENT TO SUPERFICIALITY

I've been puzzled by educators' lack of interest in generating student mastery and still await enlightenment about this. Back in the 1990s, I had assembled an early version of the approach I explain here, documented it with references, illustrated it with practical experiences, organized it into a thoughtful explanation, and obtained time with a state's commissioner of education.

She welcomed me graciously, accepted my document, and assured me she would read it. At a later appointment, she informed me that she had read it, congratulated me, told me it aligned very well with the research, handed me a detailed summary assembled by her own staff, gave mine back to me, and wished me well.

I had found the one person in the state with the most power to change education, had been told that my methods worked and aligned with what else was known, and that was the end of it. A division director there told me privately that his data showed one-third of the state's students dropping out, one-third coasting, and one-third receiving a good education.

"In other words," he concluded soberly, "our schools really serve just a third of our students."

That state used neither my approach nor its own compilation. The idea that government itself would use "the research" to alter classroom practice was of no interest. This and other experiences have led me to regard research as largely impotent, proffered usually in support of what one has decided to do anyway.

In truth, the results that concern us most are easy to understand. A rule of thumb for possessing useful knowledge is whether, when you're taking a walk, you can call it up and think about it. To do that about any issue, I know exactly the activity that prepares me for it, and you probably do also.

What a student can explain to you correlates with how much he or she is able to think about it. Engage students in conversation about a subject they've had and say, "I'm interested. Tell me everything." Then compare the number of *minutes* of knowledge they have with the number of *months* they spent studying it.

In my own K–12 schooling spanning the middle of the last century, a few teachers were "old school," expecting comprehensive knowledge, and others weren't. Among the latter was my sophomore year world history teacher, who took us through hundreds of pages of small print in our text. As the end of the term loomed, a courageous student asked him, "Mr. X, what are we going to have on our final exam?"

"Don't worry," he said, smiling benevolently. "Before the test we'll go over some review questions."

Everyone leaned back, looked at each other, and grinned broadly. What in prior decades would have been teacher-complicit cheating was now cutting-edge methodology. The point wasn't what you actually knew but that you passed the checkpoint, and the school would help you do that. Bad grades on finals would reflect on the school also. Set up a favorable environment, let osmosis do the work, and teachers needn't stress students by requiring sustained learning.

EXTRACT WHAT TO SAVE

Good experiences can enliven learning, but while they may be entertaining, we need to notice what makes them educative. They should enable us to do later something we couldn't do before. A new ability, a new perspective, comes under our personal management. The educative element may not be obvious so we must reflect on it, sort out what's worth saving, and install it explicitly. How would we re-create this experience for someone else?

Once I visited a district's demonstration school, wandering from room to room, and as the day wound down entered the kindergarten. The room was fragrant with the smell of freshly baked bread. The day had been taken up with making and eating it, but the children were restless. They'd "had a good experience" but needed something more.

Imagine them going home and saying to their mother, "I know how to make Swedish rye bread!" *and actually doing so*. By the end of the day the experience was well embedded in their physical senses and vivid in their imagination. The plan stood before them on two easels where the teacher had neatly printed out the ingredients and steps.

She could have ended the day saying, "Let's close our eyes now and imagine every step. Can you see the ingredients on the table? Let's make sure everyone can tell all of them, and all the steps." They'd have reached home prepared to demonstrate proudly.

Why wouldn't a teacher spontaneously take the experience to that level?

I believe it's from misunderstanding the function of conscious knowledge. If you assume that an activity itself is enough, then you needn't select details to remember deliberately. Children often seem so invested in what they do that we think they will automatically retain it. Yet if we lean too much on osmosis and don't mine the experience deliberately, they're more likely to lose it: "The bread at home didn't turn out like it did at school, so which ingredient did I forget?"

To do anything in the world or even to understand it, we refer to our mental plan. When the teacher's guiding hand is removed from our shoulder and we must soldier on by ourselves, we consult our idea. If we retain nothing consciously, even though we obeyed the hand, we're helpless and lost, which describes many dropouts—confused, unsure they can learn, and haphazard with their mental resources. How many who leave are certain and proud of knowledge they've mastered? Schools need to extricate themselves from the goo of vague learning and intend for students actually to know what they know.

PAVLOV'S ADVICE

People who use knowledge properly can help guide us. A line from Ivan Pavlov that I've carried for decades provides a model: "A scientist must accustom himself to the gradual accumulation of knowledge." Several threads apply to our discussion.

- *Scientist*—This could be anyone who expects to have an intellectual life or to manage him- or herself by deliberately acquired knowledge. We should find this quality in anyone who claims to be educated.
- *Must*—Inevitability arises not from an arbitrary mandate but from the nature of knowledge. To have a life of the mind, we can't avoid this step.
- *Accustom*—One commits to a habit, a manner of proceeding, with all knowledge, rather than to a random or sporadic event. We do away with hurry and pressure, and send roots into the task like a marathon runner rather than a sprinter.
- *Gradual*—Knowledge patiently builds one facet upon another. We can't proceed to the refined until the simple adorns our mind, a process that can only be the steady activity of years.
- *Accumulation*—This means not just obtaining an idea and discarding it to find another, but obtaining, keeping, and building on what's retained. B after A, C after B. If one reaches L-M-N having discarded A-B-C, one starts over and nothing accumulates.

Pavlov made important contributions apart from the study of conditioned reflexes for which he is best known, and was the first Russian to win a Nobel Prize (Physiology/Medicine, 1904). From a lifetime in science, shortly before his death in 1936 he summed up his thinking for the young scientists of Russia about whom he cared deeply. Important for us is that his view is a polar opposite to what's governed K–12 education here for three-quarters of a century. He wrote:

What can I wish to youth who devote themselves to science? Firstly, gradualness. About this most important condition of fruitful scientific work I never can speak without emotion. Gradualness, gradualness, and gradualness. From the very beginning of your work, school yourselves to severe gradualness in the accumulation of knowledge.

Learn the ABC of science before you try to ascend to its summit. Never begin the subsequent without mastering the preceding. Never attempt to screen an insufficiency of knowledge even by the most audacious surmise and hypotheses. Howsoever this soap-bubble will rejoice your eyes by its play, it inevitably will burst and you will have nothing except shame.

School yourselves to demureness and patience. Learn to inure yourselves to drudgery in science. Learn, compare, collect the facts! Perfect as is the wing of a bird, it never could raise the bird up without resting on air. Facts are the air of a scientist. Without them you can never fly. Without them your "theories" are vain efforts.

But learning, experimenting, observing, try not to stay on the surface of the facts. Do not become the archivists of facts. Try to penetrate to the secret of their occurrence, persistently search for the laws which govern them.

Secondly, modesty. Never think that you already know all. However highly you are appraised, always have the courage to say of yourself—I am ignorant.

Do not allow haughtiness to take you in possession. Due to that you will be obstinate where it is necessary to agree, you will refuse useful advice and friendly help, you will lose the standard of objectiveness.

Thirdly, passion. Remember that science demands from a man all his life. If you had two lives that would not be enough for you. Be passionate in your work and your searchings.[7]

Pavlov suggests *encounter, learn, remember, expand, apply,* and *care.* The typical school sequence is *encounter, learn, forget,* and *start over.* The first is organized around the determination to assimilate comprehensive, permanent, usable knowledge. The second surrenders after obtaining familiarity.

THREE EFFORTS

Although you're directed to methods that produce familiarity, mastery is only a skip and jump further. *Saving* is the turning point. Once the knowledge is obtained, the mastery model distinguishes what to save from it and how to do that. The steps are under teachers' control, doable, and an acceptable use of class time.

We *install knowledge.* The first word is *activity* and the second *content*: Do the first to the second. Such an intent hour by hour affords a valid way to measure success. It's what we expect of ourselves when we tell someone we know something, and also aligns with what the big tests and society ultimately require. It also truly satisfies students—their own mastery, their own competence. We achieve familiarization and speed on past it with three distinct efforts:

1. *Selecting what to save.* Once students access knowledge, we distinguish what's worth saving from what needs only to be understood, and we put in hard copy what we select.
2. *Practicing it to save it.* To engage long-term memory, we arrange for students to practice and assimilate what we identify. They bring learning into short-term memory by our presentation, recall it at once to assure an accurate initial impression (explained to a partner or written down), and then repeatedly reconstitute or reconsolidate it at expanding time intervals (recalled later).
3. *Demonstrating it steadily instead of rarely or never.* We enable students to perform and display their knowledge daily.

Our aim is to bring all learning up to this standard of mastery: *the ability to call up deliberately what one has learned and maintain it.*

The standard has three aspects, one customary and two not. The familiar one is "call up what one has learned." Students do this when they answer a question or take a test. So far, so good. If they do even this much, most negotiate the checkpoints, though their learning may be temporary.

The other two aspects are less familiar. "Deliberately" implies learning deeply enough that it's under students' conscious control. They don't guess nor depend on a question that supplies most of the answer. They cease to rely on hints, scaffolding, clues, or question design and do more than transfer information from one piece of paper to another.

"Deliberate" implies enough mastery to tell whether a point is complete, better in this spot or that, now or later, coupled with one nuance or another; and the confidence to bring it up at will in any setting. It expands the idea of "calling up" so it becomes the skilled expression of well-mastered learning.

Those two steps transform learning, but we can take it further to permanence with a third element that alters the game entirely: "and maintain it." We ask students to *maintain* "the skilled expression of well-mastered learning," saving it, turning knowledge into a continuing inner resource.

This intent is indispensable for accumulating knowledge yet is disclaimed as a school responsibility. "Students can do this themselves if they wish," goes the thinking. "It's not our job." Saying this, the school *obstructs* the retention of knowledge. By its courses, credits, review questions, cramming, and final exams, the system informs students unmistakably, "Drop this and go to the next thing."

You may object that you don't have time for what I suggest, but—to be honest—don't you make time for what you consider important? If saving knowledge is even the point of it all, you put this first in your use of time and achieve what students intuitively regard as success: to master something and be able to demonstrate it anytime.

We know students are at this point when they can explain a connected series of ideas, appropriately place details in context, think a train of thought about the subject, follow out an idea using only what's in their mind, and engage in intelligent conversation about it. A nearly infallible sign of genuine learning is wanting to talk about it with others who possess parallel knowledge.

To apply this chapter, sort out your uses of time. Give each a name and separate them into two groups—those leading to long-term retention of knowledge and those not. Plan how you can employ more of the first and fewer of the second.

SUMMARY

1. Schools typically fail to make learning permanent piece by piece.
2. The goal instead is to get students past checkpoints.
3. A widespread ten-factor "learn-and-lose" system actively extinguishes learning.
4. After students apprehend knowledge on the surface, they need to save it in depth.
5. U.S. education has not deliberately determined that students will save knowledge.
6. The problem began with progressive education's dismissal of academic mastery.
7. We have instead a systemic commitment to temporarily familiar knowledge.
8. Teachers need to specify exactly what is worth the continued effort to save it.
9. Pavlov: "A scientist must accustom himself to the gradual accumulation of knowledge."
10. We need to select what to save, save it, and periodically demonstrate it.
11. Mastery: the ability to call up deliberately what one has learned and maintain it.

THREE

Practice Requires Effort: The Essential Place of Focused Effort

Our two levers are teacher effort and student effort. The first must direct the second and, to transform schools, must do so differently than occurs now.

Whatever adults do about education—buildings they build, laws they pass, money they allocate, teachers they train—all that activity must result somehow in *students doing something different.* Contrary to the assumptions of progressive education, they learn only by means of their effort. No matter what "song and dance" teachers perform, great experiences they arrange, or fascinating thing they present, it must take hold in the effort of students who, unless guided differently, exert as little of it as possible.

ASSESS THEIR EFFORT

There are several ways to plot what happens now:

1. Take a quiet place in a classroom and focus just on this issue. Time students in two categories, Overall Working and Overall Not Working, the time-on-task factor. Their proportion of time in each will probably correlate with their academic achievement both individually and as a class.
2. Usually it's the one talking who exerts effort. Teachers are urged to aim for students to do 70 to 80 percent of the talk in class, but experience indicates that that proportion better describes teacher talk, creating a huge hole in student effort. To learn more deeply, students would have to override the teacher.

15

3. Pick a student, follow him or her around for a day, and with a stopwatch add up time reasonably labeled "effort." Ask whether, after each use of time, the student has advanced his or her mastered knowledge, such as by taking notes, reading, writing, or concentrating in some way. Effort will likely mark less than half the time, with much instead spent distracted or in activity neutral to sustained learning such as processing educational materials without effort, waiting for the next thing to happen, aimless conversation, writing notes to friends, playing, and communicating with others nonverbally. Boredom, on average, will probably be the dominant feeling.

4. Watch students after a teacher presents a lesson. While good discussions can stretch their understanding and involve everyone, those that are teacher led often insulate students from effort. If one happens to know an answer or catch a thread of reasoning and supply the right word to a question, it takes him or her all of fifteen seconds.

   Others are both grateful and passive: "Good. He's keeping the teacher busy." They first want to be sure they don't embarrass themselves—achieved by remaining silent. Accomplishing that, they next want to show up well, and without realizing it, teachers may give most attention to those who do. Center stage are the active ones who like to perform, while the remainder drift. As knowledge passes their brains, the latter don't expect to grapple with it.

5. If your students might be anywhere in this picture, find out for sure with a timer. Get hard data. Time how long they actually try to do something that challenges their mind. Observe their collective behavior at random moments and ask yourself, "Is this effort at learning?" Four out of five times your answer may be no.

Effort is energy exerted toward a purpose. Think how you personally experience that—how it feels. You spur yourself with the thought, "I'm getting somewhere. I'm moving to what I want." You notice a satisfying internal force and experience yourself as *efficacious*, having substance, possessing power over a part of your environment. If someone asked you, "What are you trying to do now?," you could tell them. Fundamental to this is the conviction that your goal just then is *right*. Doubts about it sap energy while certainty redoubles it.

The sense I get instead from many classrooms is that students are mainly waiting. They wait for the next task they must respond to, wait to be able to talk to the person they really want to relate to, wait for school to let out, wait to go to the restroom, or wait for some unknown force to stimulate them. Something outside them must pick up their attention and focus it. If given a direction for their labor, they find no energy in it.

Seeing them bored or frustrated or waiting for you to guide them reveals that they have no personal direction for their energy. Without it, they will just survive, get through the day with as little damage to their self-esteem as they can. They need a personal intent to increase their knowledge and a way to channel their effort to accomplish that.[8]

AN EPIPHANY

It took me a long time to understand how purposeful exertion applies in the classroom. After twenty years of working with classroom methods, an epiphany in 1992 changed everything.

At the time, my son was in a middle school soccer league. I knew each of his teammates, by and large average students uninterested in academics. On a rainy Saturday as I watched them plunge about a muddy field, I was impressed at how motivated they were, but then compared this with what I knew of their classroom effort. Since it was the same boy both here and there, I realized that the difference lay in the conditions applied by the rules of soccer and the team interaction on the one hand, and the atmosphere, expectations, and tasks communicated by the teacher in the classroom on the other.

To appreciate this requires causal thinking. Causes at work on the playing field were missing from the classroom. One setting created excitement and the other boredom, so what made the difference? Understanding this preoccupied me for fifteen years, and in 2007 I published an explanation of methods to turn around or accelerate any classroom and obtain sustained academic mastery (republished under the title *A Compendium of Methods: Practice Makes Permanent*).

Activities address both curricular knowledge and affective needs. With simple steps students can express their ideas, build thinking together, master a spectrum of communication skills, remember what's said, give total attention to another, and discuss relevant topics openly.

APPLYING EFFORT

Learning such things takes effort, a type of purposeful exertion common to both academic and behavioral change: *focusing on the relevant point of knowledge*. With behavior, change in students' conduct can occur just by the accurate application of effort for seconds at a time.

As I developed the checklist for communication skills that appears in the book noted above, I tried many combinations to find the best set. Heading the list was just the idea of listening to another speak, but I soon discovered that a type of effort preceded even this.

My students were surprised to realize that *waiting their turn required effort*. It took effort to sustain the discomfort of restraining a response they wanted to make. It took effort to focus outwardly on what another was saying instead of inwardly on what they were preparing to say. Once one becomes consciously aware of such effort, however, it's easy to apply. You know the difficulty you cope with and plan for the action due.

Both behavior and learning depend, in other words, on where effort makes a difference. Often it lies just in changing a thought, reinterpreting a situation. A physically talented nine-year-old I knew was conscious of his superior agility. He typically wanted to win at anything he tried, and when frustrated would become enraged and confront another student nose to nose as though saying, "I'm going to clean up the playground with you." While he never threw fists, he could intimidate other students to do his bidding.

I thought about his cognitive error. What was his unproductive thinking, and how could he apply effort to change it? I let him know how I appreciated his varied skills so he saw me as supportive.

Standing beside him quietly one day, I said, "I think I know how you can solve a problem really quickly." He looked at me with interest and I continued, "Just tell yourself, 'I can solve this problem without getting mad.'"

Here was a reassessment of the situation ("I want to solve a problem" in place of "Others are making me unhappy") and an action step ("I can dismiss anger"). Apparently this was on target because in the next month I saw him angry only once. Even competitive activity didn't upset him. He would throw himself into a game and let it turn out as it might.

"I notice you haven't been getting mad," I said to him later. "What are you doing differently?"

"I just let it go," he replied with a smile.

An instant of effort can produce a marked change, but it must be precisely applied. Staff had often admonished him about his behavior to no effect. Their attempts were unfocused, not attached to the specific way in which his mind directed his personal effort.

While physical effort develops more physical skill, effort in learning accumulates a body of knowledge. Pavlov was eloquent about this in his letter to young scientists (see chapter 2), and the logic of his advice is inescapable. A cognitive edifice rests on basic layers.

EXPAND THE FOCUS OF EFFORT

The change needed in the focus of effort can be expressed diagrammatically: Exert effort to learn words, and they come together in sentences. Save the sentences, and they turn into paragraphs. Then paragraphs become sections, sections become chapters, and chapters add up to a book. Do this with one subject after another, and you have an education.

Important about this sequence is that a novel task of mastery occurs *at each successive dimension*. One doesn't master the chapter, in other words, just by learning all the sentences. Once the sentences are learned, we face a different chunk size to ingest. Assimilation depends on understanding from a new level.

So far I haven't encountered anyone as excited as I was about that sequence when I first stumbled upon it eighteen years ago. I was certain that if people would just hear it out, they could transform their schools *because it spells out where to aim student effort.* The progression still appears inescapable to me. Mastery of the whole awaits assimilation of parts. Between the sentences at one end and the chapter at the other is effort at accumulation. There's no shortcut.

That this sequence is ignored explains a common problem. Because increasing chunk size is meant to build upon a prior acquisition, if it doesn't, even exhaustive effort may show poor results. Teachers and students work hard for so little progress because they violate the cumulative nature of the brain's organization and assimilation of knowledge.

Learning one sentence after another doesn't add up to learning the subject. Students must grasp the paragraph at the paragraph level, the section at the section level, and the subject at the subject level—thinking like authors do when they write the textbook.

When I was in high school, I helped my father build a four-apartment building in the lot beside our house. I recall being awestruck at the mountain of lumber delivered all at once as we started. We had all the pieces in our possession, but resting in a pile they were a far cry from a completed building.

ASSIGNMENTS

In general, the more practice effort students apply to paper-bound assignments, the more familiarity they gain. One of the best things I did in my formal education was taking notes from lectures and books and writing a summary of them. Teachers do students a service by challenging them with genuine issues to ponder and write about or giving them chunks of information to organize and summarize. Feedback afterward enhances the value of the writing. Though time consuming, writing-and-feedback sets learning on a superior track.

A different kind of assignment is less useful—moving information from one place to another (screen to paper, book to paper, screen to screen, or one part of a paper to another). Students look up something, run it through required motions, and turn it in. Based on what we've said, what's missing? No advancing assimilation of the knowledge is expected.

If they forget all about the assignment, throw away their papers, and never think about it again, *this is acceptable*. They've exercised their brain briefly to rearrange data, the assignment registers scattershot in working memory, and long-term memory receives almost nothing.[9]

A criterion to apply to any assignment is whether the work product is worth saving. Start back with a first grade class distinguishing rocks— igneous, sedimentary, and metamorphic. They learn the names, and with a few pictures and stories put more words to their understanding. Then they reach into the class's box of rock samples and sort them. They remember, explain, and apply.

Their next sixteen years of school may not improve on the knowledge of rocks they gain in the first grade. As curriculum designers invent lessons, in other words, they can draw on legitimate knowledge. In grasping numbers and letters, why not combine them with growing knowledge about people, ideas, and the world? Why not learn about real things the mind will continue to use for a lifetime instead of make-work sample sentences not worth another glance? Identifying rocks isn't the only solid learning worth a second glance from a first grader.

This criterion was on my mind as I interviewed a high school junior who wanted to transfer to the small school I operated for a time. She'd given up on the public system and came to me for a different way to get an education, and I would asked her to bring what she had been working on. She drew from her backpack an inch-thick sheaf of papers, said, "These are from English," and dropped them in my wastebasket.

"Wait a minute!" I protested. "There must be something worth saving!" If you put effort into learning, I expected, some of it deserves carrying forward.

"No," she said, "there isn't," and shook her head dismally.

I retrieved the pages later and examined them one by one. She was right. Nothing was worth saving—which I cannot recall without sorrow. With centuries of world literature available, her school occupied her study of it with what deserved to be thrown away.

What was true about her assignments appears to be the big downside to most. Either there's nothing worth saving in them or they're discarded anyway. We run student minds through an assignment, they get what they can, and then we drop it and go on.

Perhaps teachers make an unwarranted leap from the usefulness of math assignments. My guess is that those work because (1) the effort is specifically defined, (2) it builds on something from before, and (3) the learning is reused later. Comparably in other subjects, the value of the questions at the end of the chapter probably depends on whether the knowledge in them continues to be drawn upon, which may not occur systematically.

Teachers instead take comfort that they've caused students to focus at least briefly on a point, and students receive a piece of paper to verify that the teacher, at least, has covered the curriculum. The outcome too often is the familiarity we noted above that stands in place of, and gives the passing impression of, mastery.

Many assignments also diverge from the central curricular material. Each student may be asked to work on something different, but because their work isn't common to all it doesn't receive follow-up and testing with the material in common. The paper dropped in the basket by the assigned hour is accorded credit though it receives zero attention later. With the assignment completed and credit assigned, what more, the teacher thinks, could possibly be done?

LOSS OF LONG-TERM MEMORY

Please. *Focus.* The point of education is what goes into long-term memory, not into working memory that constantly discards its contents to accommodate the incoming. Are we together on that at least? In the assignment is a quantity of student effort resulting in knowledge traced at least once onto short-term memory. It deserves identification and preservation, and it needn't be identical student to student.

The step due is that students retain and be accountable for the substance they gather. What they realize instead is that the teacher's dismissal of completed work tells them what to do with it themselves. They're taught to exert learning effort but not hold onto anything as a result.

A unique study helped illuminate the astonishing outcome of the learn-and-discard pattern endemic to mainstream education. Years ago, *Scientific American* published an article titled "Teaching Real Science," a review of how high schools deliver science instruction. One study concerned 12,000 high school students, half of whom had had a biology course and half of whom had not, aiming to discover the difference in their knowledge of biology.

From the detailed nature of the subject, one might assume that the two groups would separate cleanly, that it would be easy to tell which a student belonged to, and that the worst course-taker would still be clearly better than the best non-course-taker.

Yet the jaw-dropping conclusion noted by the *Scientific American* author was that "half of those who had never taken a course in biology did as well in tests as 40% of those who had: apparently biology courses taught most of those taking them almost nothing." By looking at the score of almost half the number, *you couldn't tell whether they'd had the course or not.*[10]

Hold this picture in mind while you remember your own fearsome effort if you took high school biology and yet how little you retained. If you didn't aim at cumulative retention, even after your hard work so much information evaporated. It did so *predictably*, in fact, because such an outcome is structured into the brain.

When we receive new material, learn it poorly, and then overlay more on top of it, the brain goes into triage, literally extinguishing prior knowledge: "Drop all that. Alligators incoming." This isn't due to students' inattention. The instructional design itself interdicts the revisiting and recall that generates retention deep enough to withstand the impact of new material.

I contrast this with my daughter's high school biology course from an excellent Seattle teacher who expected students to retain what they learned. One day, he took them to a remote beach and instructed them to find every living creature they could and learn its Latin name. At a parent evening, I asked him why he did that.

"It gives them confidence in their knowledge," he told me. My daughter, now a marine biologist, says she has often used what she learned in his course. Whatever the initial experience or input is, a single further step preserves its value. Subject all material to cumulative recall. Aim all learning effort toward permanent mastery.

For a professional educator, this idea should not be aquiver with cognitive dissonance. For a time during my education, I took several courses with the same classmates. Most of us followed curiosity to do outside reading while one of our number, named Reuben, spent his spare time mastering prior courses.

Soon it was clear who had made the better choice. A question would come up and no one would know the answer. Someone would say, "Go ask Reuben. He'll know," and he would. Ever since, I've valued his model as an avenue to mastery. Just make sure you don't forget what you labored to learn; Reubenize it.

THE COOKIE PRINCIPLE

We allot effort better if we recognize how underlying regularity makes it easy. Follow me here in what occurs when you bake cookies. There's system, there's pattern to it. You carry out certain actions much the same every time while varying other ingredients and steps.

The cookie principle is that if you can bake a dozen cookies, you can bake a thousand dozen. Reproduce the standard elements, vary the variables, and repeat as needed. You want to walk a thousand steps and know how to walk one? No problem. Do the one a thousand times.

An old documentary about Chinese road building showed an army of men with shovels and buckets: If you can move dirt a bucket at a time and the hill contains a million buckets, no problem. Move them one at a time. The principle tells you to understand the repeated behavior that eventually solves the problem *and repeat it.* Identify the salient effort and do it over and over. To improve, know the crucial activities and keep doing them.

Student needs call out urgently for the cookie principle. I worked for a time with five immigrant students new to a charter school. They ranged in age from eleven to fifteen and had been in the United States one to six years. Although all were already fluent in speaking and understanding English, they *read and wrote at the kindergarten to second grade level.* Despite years in the U.S. system, they couldn't function in age-level classes.

How could this be? Like no other subject, language learning depends on practice. It can be efficient or inefficient but can't be avoided. That they read at the K–2 level meant that their prior schools failed to use the cookie principle and did not identify and require the key effort. Each student first needed personal guidance even to unlock the code translating the shape and sound of letters into words. No one had supplied this.

Once having the code, they could at least begin to teach themselves and draw from help. Their learning program should have seen them practicing the key knowledge morning till night. Instead they got group classes where they faked, imitated, and guessed at answers but learned nearly nothing for their one to six years in the U.S. system. Whoever taught them failed doubly—both to identify the effort that made practice possible and then to guide them to do it.

Consider the alternative to practice. *There is none!* We can't improve at a sport without practice and can't pump knowledge into students around or despite or without their effort. We have to *use* their effort, and how we guide them to do it spells success or failure. We do it poorly and they learn poorly. We do it well and they learn well.

The rings of influence around them—peers, classroom, teacher, school, district, state, federal government, and the apparatus of regulation and control—aren't good starting points. Our success in dealing with these rings in their due time depends on the organizing principle they serve. What comes ahead of what? What do we put first and make sure we don't screw up?

If we make anything central that really isn't, we guarantee underserving what's truly important. One event millions of times daily causes learning—the active intersection of a child's mind with knowledge. We have to understand it and arrange the conditions that sustain it.

You of course adapt your content, presentation, discussion, assignments, and tests. If you've made cookies, you know many variations are possible as long as a few repeated things are done right. Everything can be varied except what you need to do the same. What, for instance, is the recipe for making knowledge permanent?

REPEATED RECALL

Can we agree on the fact that *there's only one answer to this question*, even though it can be done in different ways? Students must call up the knowledge again and again. They assimilate the old with optimum periodicity of repetition, integrating new with old, and using different ways to express it.

With the old well in hand, you add new learning with assurance. You maintain the prior body of knowledge even while making it rich and growing it in students' minds, and show how the current integrally extends the preceding. As you tinker with their grasp of it, the amount of practice they exert, and their other uses of mind, you improve at predicting accurately the progress they make from minutes spent.

If you don't know where effort makes a difference, you can't practice it successfully no matter how much you want to. Semibewildered little people aren't going to figure this out. Steering their attention into the groove where practice matters is up to us.

Once I was standing in an elementary school library when a boy came up to the counter with a large stack of books. I recognized him as the subject of conversation among the teachers. He misbehaved, and they worried about him. He smiled fleetingly at the librarian, pushed toward her the books he wanted, and said, "I'm *really* going to try hard."

His comment cut me to the heart. He was in trouble—adults were down on him—he wanted to change, had no clue what to alter in his world, and seized on the only thing he could think of—checking out books to read. Indeed he needed to exert effort, but what? Was it enough just to try any old thing? No, there were specifics. For the school, certain conditions were critical, but they weren't in his mind. No one focused his effort.

You can extend this to any learning in depth. Apply students' effort so they get somewhere. The criterion you answer to is their permanence of knowledge. In six months, will they retain what you teach? If with no warning you gave a comprehensive test about what they learned two months ago, how would they do? About current material, what would they answer spontaneously tomorrow, and how long do you expect them to retain it?

SUMMARY

1. We ultimately progress only by student effort.
2. Students currently put out far less effort than they could and usually are waiting.
3. Students expend effort in sports because of the conditions.
4. Different conditions in the classroom quash student energy.

5. Behavior change requires applying certain effort, even if briefly.
6. Students must apply effort to learn successive levels of a subject.
7. Assignments are less useful as students "run through the motions" and get credit.
8. The point of education is what passes from working memory into long-term memory.
9. Students who had never taken a biology course scored as well as 40 percent of those who had taken one.
10. Students should expect to retain everything from prior courses.
11. If you can bake a dozen cookies, you can bake a thousand dozen. Repeat essential actions.
12. Successful effort leads to long-term retention.

FOUR

Effort in the Inner Venue: Connect Learning to Effort inside the Mind

Learning depends on effective effort. We have two kinds to choose from. One field is accessible to the senses—the outer or visible. The other isn't and rests solely on thinking. Since the results we want must turn up in the invisible venue, we can surmise that effort must lie there as well. We need to know *what kind of efforts in the inner venue make a difference.* Here are six.

1. FOCUSING

Directing attention to a specific point enables the mind to receive an impression of knowledge through reading, listening to another, or direct experience. Focusing is usually taken for granted and performed unconsciously, but in truth it takes effort. One way is to "defocus," to turn away from one thing toward something else. Another is to "refocus," to change from a scattered or aimless mind to return to a prior idea.[11]

We want students to know what they're doing with their minds so they can draw on it efficiently. We want them to practice its conscious management thoroughly enough that they can do it together and with confidence and group order.

2. CALLING UP MEMORY

Everyone recognizes the value of this effort when facing an examination. We rehearse our memories until we know we can serve up what's likely to be asked. Remembering gets an idea into students' heads so that they can do something else with it. To find out if they're successful at it, schools use the standard means. They ask questions. They verify or validate learning with questions large and small, with understanding or without it, superficially or in depth. The prevalence of this practice tells us how enthusiastic U.S. education is about it even though the emphasis can be misplaced. Our intent in using questions shouldn't be just to assess students but rather to deepen their knowledge.

3. SUPPLYING WORDS TO IMPRESSIONS

This effort moves learning from "I think I get it" to "Here's how I'd explain it." Until they're recast in words, initial impressions usually remain disorganized and poorly installed in the mind. Passing from an early impression, gained from the external presentation, to the student's own redesign of it, written or spoken, we engage a wider meaning network. Much of learning involves new terminology, but to be understood the terms need to be linked to other words, symbols, or objects already grasped.

A different way to note the difficulty is to begin in the outer environment with tangible images or words in print, picture, or sound. These tangible elements stand before a mind *that isn't tangible,* and the bridge between the two remains elusive. Somehow the mind swallows sensory impressions and manages to convert them into networks of association.

Leaving aside subconscious and unconscious representations of reality, we make conscious knowledge usable by integrating the new impression word by word with what we already know. Attempting to nail down an elusive idea, we say to someone, "Let me get this straight. You're saying that . . ." and arrange our own brain's data notes into a meaning field. Information receiving no such processing gains haphazard purchase.

4. ARRANGING IDEAS TO MAKE SENSE

Quality of learning rises further when you achieve the first three steps of focus, memory, and expression in words *and then try to make sense to other people.* An occasion to explain drives thought toward the connection between ideas. Higher stages of knowledge presume this. Anyone who expects to be turned loose to practice a profession knows that the closer they get to certification, the more they must exchange ideas with teachers and other learners. In every expertise, the sharing between those who know many of the same things powerfully affects the development of learners' thinking.

We might expect that as teachers declare students educationally competent, self-defense alone would drive them to intimate familiarity with students's thoughts. Will they do so much harm later that people come back to check who taught them? We want to know if loose ball bearings skew this person's judgment or if ignorance of presumed knowledge will generate mistakes and malpractice.

We find out only by personal challenge to their thought in a setting where students can say what's on their mind and others can respond. All this can occur only after students master common knowledge about a subject. We begin, in other words, with retaining a basic fund of knowledge, but then must probe each one's use of it.

5. RECHUNKING

This activity gathers bits of knowledge into coherent sets that can be used like a single thought so that the mental process proceeds faster by larger steps. In chapter 3 I noted learning as moving naturally from sentences to paragraphs to sections to chapters and so on. If learning is comprehensive, *the mind can deal with chunks at any of those levels*. With increased skill at anything, you find that with one command you can order a more complex action, drawing fully on prior levels of learning. This principle is particularly important for systematic intellectual development.

Reading follows this pattern. First come sounds of individual letters, laboriously negotiated one at a time. After practicing them awhile, our eye soon blends the sounds into combinations and then into whole words absorbed automatically. Similarly a student learning geometry can soon recognize at a glance the structure of a set of data and instantly estimate an answer that before would have taken several steps. Such reconditioning results in faster and more accurate thought. The more of it we obtain, the freer is our conscious mind to proceed to other tasks, a freedom achieved only by practice.

After several years of working at drums, my son became proficient at them. I inquired of him once what it meant to have advanced skill in drumming. He pointed out in a particular piece how two timings occurred simultaneously—a noticeable beat in the music but also a subtle one that bound it together through longer intervals not obvious to the ear. It would take long practice, he said, to condition the mind to accommodate both rhythms simultaneously, but that top drummers could do this.

In practicing a musical instrument, a stream of subtle possibilities enters awareness—softer here, faster here, more carefully there, and so on. As internal activity is integrated, conscious guidance can employ unconscious portions. The mind takes in hand certain multistep processes and commands the whole thing, leaving attention available to modify the few details it wishes to tinker with.

An Example from Mathematics

A colleague described Nobel Prize winner Richard Feynman's mathematical ability as almost magical. He could focus on a problem intensely for a few moments and then declare the correct answer, essentially skipping the intermediate steps that even expert mathematicians would follow.

Yet this was a developed capacity. He had practiced so many mathematical processes so thoroughly that he could command his unconscious mind to perform them. In his engaging autobiography, one follows a curious mind constantly practicing its ability against problems in the real world.[12] Few people take up safecracking as an entertaining mathematical challenge.

A Sports Illustration

Hillary Lindh, a resident of my hometown, won the gold medal for women's downhill skiing in the World Cup races of 1997 among many other lifetime achievements. From the time she was belt high, she hurtled past astonished adult skiers, leaving behind "another Hillary Lindh story."

I watched her gold medal run with interest, wondering how her mind worked, since at seventy to ninety miles an hour almost every act must be done automatically. There's no time to weigh which command to give which muscle to adapt to a new detail. The command chunks must be in place already for them to be used at the speed required.

An event occurred during her run that commentators afterward noted as the moment she won the race. Near its end, the course came over a lip that dropped away sharply. Most skiers went airborne so that their bodies lengthened, slowing their time. Hillary, probably thirty feet before the brow, raised her skis under her and was already descending when she reached it. She skied in a tuck for the time others were floating, shaving microseconds off her time.

Think of this in terms of rechunking. How much practice would it take to fulfill all other demands automatically in order to free her mind to gauge exactly when to make that adjustment? Whatever the quality of that practice is, it distinguishes a gold medalist from others. Practice binds together a constellation of data into a network that hangs together by multiple threads so that one can enter it from any angle and remain perfectly oriented.

An Example from Academia

Browsing TV channels, I happened upon a Harvard professor lecturing to a couple thousand students about the development of law in prior centuries. Working without notes, he was able to present an idea, pose a probing question about what he had said, entertain answers from anywhere in the lecture hall, comment upon them, and resume progress through his sequence of ideas.

He was obviously master of a subject, a skill achieved only by long practice at input and output. Bit by bit he rechunked the subject so that he could draw creatively on entire integrated pieces.[13]

6. CONCENTRATING

This is the graduate level of focusing. Albert Einstein provided a standard. He said he had developed the ability to focus on one thing without a single distractive thought for up to forty-two minutes, which he accomplished by determined practice from his youth. He placed a pad of paper beside his work. Whenever he experienced a divergent thought, he would say, "I will not allow that to distract me again," and make a tally on the pad to plot his progress. Because it annoyed him to do this, it constituted a motive to improve.[14]

Two aspects are crucial for students. One is to understand the kind of effort required and the other is self-checking on its use. Ask students to rate themselves on two measures for any given period: (1) the number of minutes spent in study activity and (2) their level of concentration in that time on a percentage scale. Then multiply the integers.

A student spending forty minutes at 10 percent concentration would score 400 concentration units (CUs), but with fifty minutes at 80 percent would score 4,000 CUs. With a minor shift in time but a major one in focus, the period probably becomes ten times more useful. The first student depends entirely on what others do toward him while the second directs his own mind.

I've found that student estimates of their concentration align well with my observation of them. They know perfectly well when they're dogging it and compare themselves to others nearby. Posting their self-report publicly spurs their concentration because they like to measure themselves as getting better.

How often should you use these six kinds of internal effort?

To answer, notice if other activities accomplish your goals better. If these are the most efficient ways to spend time, you can safely fill the entire day with them. That all students at all ages and in all subjects need them suggests how basic they are and the loss to learning if they're omitted.

Repetition is common to them though sometimes discounted as automatic or unthinking reiteration. With some skills this is desired because the aim is to train the unconscious. The instruction to the physical body in shooting a basket in the gym or taking a mogul on the ski slope is barely in one's awareness. A "Do this" command engages latent chunks of knowledge given meaning and order by prior practice.

Yet experts in any field are always *thinking* about the nuances that represent improvement. They observe a principle that applies throughout civilization: *Organize the lower so the higher can flow freely.* As the more basic becomes automatic, the more advanced can receive fuller attention. In learning, we organize what we already know well enough to assign it to automatic service, spontaneously dropping a mastered chunk into place in our train of thought. Students reach that stage by practicing the six inner efforts until they can perform them automatically and confidently.

SUMMARY

1. The basic inner effort is focusing attention on a point of knowledge.
2. Calling up remembered material is a crucial learning activity.
3. Supplying words to impressions defines conscious knowledge.
4. An inner yet social effort is arranging words to make sense to another.
5. We expand our mental versatility as we can think in larger chunks.
6. Practice is essential for increasing chunk size in our conscious thought.
7. Chunking up enables us to employ smaller chunks unconsciously and effortlessly.
8. The ability to concentrate greatly affects academic progress.
9. Study time in minutes x percent of concentration = concentration units.

FIVE

Practice by Explaining: The Central Role of Explaining Learning

The shift from concrete to invisible, from outer to inner, is the perennial challenge of education. We're asked to enable students' minds to transform external data into their personal model of the world. Knowledge changes from inert to active.

In adult society, expressing knowledge is typically the point of having it. What you learn doesn't stop with you. You do something to it and pass it on. That you get it from Joe, add your part, and forward it to Bill is bound to the knowledge itself. You and Joe and Bill comprise a solar system of linked energy. One constantly communicates with coworkers and supervisors about ideas related to the job.

U.S. schools appear to regard students, on the other hand, as freestanding reservoirs to be filled rather than as a social system afloat in moving knowledge. As I lean back in my chair and let my mind wander, the words "a social system afloat in moving knowledge" paint a picture of a high-energy school. Students get one assignment every morning: "Find something you don't know, learn it, and teach it to someone else. Teachers are resources to help you. Go for it!"

ACTIVITY OF EXPLAINING

Knowledge flows most readily through the activity of explaining. Central to learning, it stimulates the six kinds of effort noted in the prior chapter and organizes knowledge. Expressive output forms students' thinking in a way that "answering the odd-numbered questions at the end of the chapter" does not. Answers outside an explanatory field disappear faster, but phrased in our own words and issuing from our own thought they associate naturally with what else we know.

The common instructional approach tends to override critical aspects of thought, however. At the start, the knowledge is external to the student in the words of a teacher or text. With the context supplied from elsewhere, the student *needn't think through the context.* Since we supply the question, the student *needn't invent the question.* The answer is brief and isolated so the student *needn't associate it elsewhere.* The question and answer are offered without prior practice so the student *doesn't absorb the material deeply.* Conditions basic to assimilated thought are missing from the start.

When personalizing a thought, instead we deliberately dredge up from our own mind the context we draw on, pose the question we want to answer, and associate the answer with links we supply, and the material arises from our prior stores of knowledge, reinforcing our retention and understanding of them.

When the teacher supplies most of the supportive notes of meaning and the student finally tosses a single word into the mix, the whole set remains apart from the student's current way of describing his world. The teacher does most of the work by providing context, question, associations, and remembered data.

The students' lone contribution may be one phrase with which the teacher hopes to "get them thinking," which may or may not happen. What did they do *after* contributing? Chances are they relaxed into the comforting thought that they pleased the teacher.

If the teacher must deliver something, why not the whole field he or she drew from, taking the time actually to convey concentrated, organized, careful knowledge and expect students to assimilate it: "All right, copy this down, explain it to a partner, and master it." Though seldom done, it would open the students to a larger picture.

Often, even written notes and reports are discarded within days of their completion. Knowledge flows by, never drunk deeply. Students listen passively, survey the data, and make a few connections, but don't write, don't summarize, don't explain, and don't save. They don't use classroom time to convert information into their own field of internal, no longer paper-dependent knowledge.

Listening to students during a lunch period, it occurred to me why they don't talk about their subjects. They don't talk about them *even while learning them.* We tell them "Do your own work," and ignore the force of social relationships as a support to learning.

When students do express their thinking, they get better at it and claim it as theirs. They connect thoughts and push them deeper. A simple psychological principle operates: *We want to claim as our own what enhances us.* Mediocre competence doesn't do this, but ideas mastered and explained gain significance. An objectively important idea isn't perceived so unless it's presentable, so that ideas students don't even mention to their friends drop far down their list of priorities.

Students' limited opportunity to explain their learning shrinks further as adults take over student talk. Teachers usually see the latter as *competing* with instruction while their own talk is automatically legitimate. Varied studies and observation tend to plot teachers' talk at between two-thirds and four-fifths of the class total. Using 70 percent as a workable figure for teacher talk leaves 30 percent for students.

Thirty percent of a fifty-minute period is fifteen minutes. A class of fifteen to thirty students then has *a half minute to one minute apiece* if all participate and someone speaks every moment. Actually the confident ones talk most. Teachers find it hard to take the added time the insecure typically need, and those who need it most say nothing.

Even this dismal picture worsens due to the quality of student talk. It seldom reaches the point of explaining but instead reacts to the teacher, with perhaps 70 to 80 percent of it brief enough to qualify for Twitter and much just a single word. Students rarely have time to draw out and integrate assorted ideas.

If we want students to draw on the recesses of their own knowledge, the most direct way is to make it a social experience. We engage their talk by inviting them to explain what they know, an activity that adapts instantly to the capacities of speaker and listener. By arming them with elementary communication skills so they can talk to each other, we make the presence of a listener socially significant, stimulating the use of knowledge.

A brief experience illustrates: One day I was conversing with a couple of other mental health professionals. As we talked, I recalled an obscure article I had read that might be relevant, and though I had only its basic outline, decided to mention it.

As I narrated what I could, *my memory dredged up details missing at first*, demonstrating the response of the brain to the expectation of making sense to others. It gladly digs up dormant associations because our desire to connect to peers through sense making is so strong. It is such dredging up "all we know about this" that students are denied in K–12. If people wonder why students don't achieve higher thinking, they might notice whether they have even made room for the simply personal thinking at the beginning of the continuum.

The same kind of effort works from kindergarten to postgraduate school, from remembering a few connected points to explaining the Theory of Everything. The enduring formative influence is *the power of another person's interest in our ideas*. Our desire to make something clearer to them spurs us to draw together what we know and to push its edges.

ASK QUESTIONS

We set up explanation just by asking questions. One about personal thoughts or feelings contains both a compliment and the offer of a bond: "I expect you to have something worthy to say, and I'm here to listen to you say it." Even with familiar material, the question stimulates the speaker to reorganize it so it's understandable to the questioner.

The purpose of a sentence, Bronowski noted, is to remove the ambiguity left over from the previous sentence.[15] An explanation presumes a pending question that invites more clarity. It may draw on memory but also on abilities to associate, reason, and originate. Questions are our way of tossing the ball to students, who then respond with their best thought. Two students face each other, one asks the other a question, and they're on their way.

Not all questions are of equal value. We might assume that comprehensive understanding occurs just by learning more details, but as we've heard, "Don't lose the forest for the trees." If we know trees but not the forest, our knowledge of a tree limps because proper use always depends on context, and the context is the forest.

What kind of question, then, puts together the details and the context? Which ones lead students to rethink, re-reflect, resynthesize, and reorganize their ideas to incorporate the details into a field of understanding and master it in an elegant form?

Explain whole subjects. If small questions don't do it, consider big ones. A clue lies in how teachers learn a subject by teaching it. As they reexplain, they deepen and expand their grasp of the entire structure of the subject. Responding to a question, they can begin where they please, at the beginning or at any point along the way, because they're conscious of the entire narrative.

That goal fits students as well. We have plenty of time to make it happen, and it's what students need later, suggesting a simple K–12 curriculum spelled out on one page: *Divide the universe of knowledge into fifty categories. About each, ask the same question every year and answer it more thoroughly, incorporating everything learned before.*

Expressed in statement form, the question is "Tell all you know about history, literature, mathematics, language, climate, geography, astronomy, psychology, religion, science, art, music, human relations, family, biology, physiology, and physics. Master any regional occupational emphasis: computers, finance, automobiles, manufacturing, mechanics, electricity, farming, mining, fishing, and lumbering."

We want students to exit formal schooling with accurate, extensive, competent knowledge. Why not make it about the whole world they'll encounter as adults and how it came to be?

If that sounds like overreaching, like many another task it breaks down to simple steps. Imagine spending a whole classroom hour learning to explain just one minute's worth of knowledge resulting in, say, five minutes of new knowledge a day. Applying the cookie principle hour by hour (see chapter 3), in 180 days of the school year students would acquire 900 minutes worth of new knowledge.

Nine hundred minutes is fifteen hours. Imagine a fourth grader doing her orals in June for two days straight, explaining all she knows. It's one spoonful at a time, absorbing one minute of knowledge per hour of learn-and-save. If comprehensive knowledge is what we want, we can have it.

A comprehensive view of a total curriculum implies that anything in it is worth learning at any time, so we can take advantage of opportunities. We don't have to confine students to Point Number 39 today when Point Number 60 comes in easy reach. A structural problem in the current design is that it minimizes the significance of curiosity and opportunity. In a pat curriculum, students are dissuaded from drawing on natural enticements because anything momentarily appealing is soon plucked from their attention.

Outside school, when one exerts effort to plunge his or her mind into a subject, aspects often emerge that invite further checking: a desire to see how some particular facet turns out, noticing the link between two things and wondering how they add up, or giving one's personal design to an array of knowledge. A brilliant friend of mine, now deceased, explained that he was incapable of learning like other people did. He would have to scour through a book till he found *one thing that interested him*, and then pursue that thread until the whole book came together in his mind.

When instead the assignment is confined from the start to what's within the lines, and another increment of the same awaits beyond it, students have every reason to deaden curiosity—a denial that makes no sense in view of our overall purpose. Learning by drawing on curiosity when it's available is like picking low-hanging fruit. Take the easy stuff ready to fall into your basket instead of insisting the kid scale the tree for the fruit hardest to reach. A saying among traders applies to learning: "Bring your basket in case they shake the tree."

Treat precise knowledge differently. In trying to move learning from the surface to the interior of the mind, two kinds of knowledge require different treatment. One kind is precise. In formulas, structures, definitions, key sequences, and translations, every single note must be learned error-free by practice.

We might expect that this depends on rote memorization, but after installing the details, students need to express the point in their own words. Parroting words or numbers may not be enough. Learning math as a student in a foreign country, we would have to explicitly translate the spoken explanation of the symbols into what had meaning in our own tongue. In learning in our native tongue, the translation into our mental language is the same task but with one step less. We need exactness in recall yet assimilation into a field of word meanings.

In the second kind of knowledge, there's still a piece to retain competently, but it's not confined to perfect recall of specific words and numbers. Instead the student needs to recall accurately the substance of a point and elaborate on it. The form given to the idea can be expressed in synonymous phrases or terms, or the latitude may be wider.

Whether the knowledge is exact or variable, it needs to be consolidated into a learnable form. Let's say a teacher directs student attention to a page of text containing 350 words. Since not all of the words must be retained, selection is involved, but for what? *To proceed, we have to convert raw text into a learnable form.* We need a hard copy containing the extent of what students are to know from that page, defining it so it can be carried forward efficiently.

Teacher and students together might create a bullet-point outline or narrative summary everyone copies into their notebook. The teacher might write out both questions and answers, or students might write their own summary. In pairs they might compare notes and help each other complete a summary. Then, summary in hand, the teacher might say, "Cover your copy now and try to explain it to a partner. Listen carefully to each other and try to remember everything said."

COMBINE WITH WRITING

The hard copy plays a key role. Anytime we ask students to create, examine possibilities, try out theories, and reconfigure priorities, we presume an array of previously mastered knowledge. For retaining detailed, comprehensive knowledge over time, a complete hard copy explanation is critical. None of us expects to retain ideas long without access to a written source. If students can't return to one to correct their mistakes, the teacher must do all the correcting.

An influence follows also from *owning* a physical object. We extend the claim to what the physical object contains: "I know everything in these pages." It's hard to make the same claim to ideas just passing through our mind or scattered about a text we can't keep.

Having a complete written answer and then explaining it recodes it into a form a student can assimilate. There's a parallel with a compost heap. Adding small biodegradable pieces to it, we still must leave them there long enough for heat to dissolve them. With ideas, we break them down small enough that students can understand them but still must hold them in an active froth in the mind if assimilation is to occur.

Learning something isn't a single event. We form it so students' minds can hold onto it but then make it easy for them to return to the activity that masters it—explaining in pieces, explaining the whole, explaining at increasing intervals of time, and explaining to different people. With the idea in a sustainable form, all that remains for mastery is for them to explain it periodically.

Comprehensive hard copy *of one's own learning* followed by thorough explaining aids mental activity we regard as "higher." A challenge to recall-and-reason stimulates the mind to sift through its stores of information. What would students need to know, for instance, if you asked them, "Describe possible outcomes of the Civil War with Union forces led throughout by McClellan compared to Grant"?

They'd need (1) the character of Grant and McClellan, (2) their respective strategies, (3) how they demonstrated them in the portion of the war under their command, (4) strategies of the Confederate forces, and finally (5) how the Confederates' likely actions would interplay with the probable responses of Grant and McClellan.

Detailed, factual knowledge is presumed even to understand the question, but it demonstrates also the limited value of learning at the factual level. If we can imagine students actually using their knowledge later, they'd like to know how to extrapolate from a fact to a spectrum of reasoning. *How would our Civil War study become useful to us?*

Is it the idea of sacrificing others' lives, the need for discipline, enduring painful conditions for a long period, the chance of personality differences, the power of ideology, skill that can be trained, or character that can't? To frame an appropriate response later, the prior learning needs to be open to interpretation in alternate directions. Following out the one that fits later becomes possible only by thorough understanding capable of spelling out ideas along their relevant continua.

THE USE OF TIME IN PRACTICE

A sequence of activity aids mastery practice. The common approach appears to be: (1) Present something, (2) drill students with brief questions and answers, and (3) give a homework assignment. This usually starts them off with an initial model of the material but one absorbed only at the surface. For permanent mastery instead, this sequence might work better:

1. Present or Assign Something

Students gather it, or you present a chunk of knowledge small enough to be assimilated initially that day, preferably that hour; for example, organized into four key points. A criterion for chunk size is your sense of progress: "If everyone gets these points, the hour is a success!"

2. Before Practicing Something, Specify It

Practice depends on having specific input you want to get better at. So if a teacher talks for an hour and students go home, this isn't practice but only the first step of the cycle, input without output. Instead, you need to unify attention around what you want them to master. The easiest way to do that is *to formulate a correct hard copy of the material.* Either have a concise handout about which you say, "You're all going to learn all of this," or create a summary of the material as noted above.

3. Partners: Understand the Problem

Your input now rests on children's minds, but left to itself it will dissolve in some of them. Your logical next step is just to get it deeper. The best time to do this is immediately after you've presented it. The whole thing is present in mind, they're focused on it, and they already sense success in grasping your point.

You don't have to fight off a host of likely distractions as you corral their attention to restart later. You don't have to compete with what they were just thinking about. You don't have to do any stage setting, retracing, context creating, or reviewing to bring them to this precise point again. They're ready to take the next step, and for this *each one needs only express outwardly what just went in.*

Aim at getting everyone able at least to tell the whole piece, everything in the summary, correctly at least once. This much practice holds it for awhile, establishing an internal model that more readily can be restored to completeness. Once they have a full answer *tellable,* they have in mind what to practice to permanence. Otherwise, some lose pieces before the day is even out, ensuring that you'll have to repeat them tomorrow, wasting class time and boring those who got them right.

If you assume that you're the one who must do all the listening to their self-expression, you face the recurring challenge of time. But in your vicinity, is there any underused resource?

If you don't trust your own ability to guide student behavior, then no, there's no other resource. If you can't get students cooperating enough to supply good attention to each other, you're out of luck. But if you've often given instructions they follow, you can tap them. They can do the job because it's easy and meets their social needs. Tell them:

> Take turns. Explain completely to your partner what we just went over. When you can each give a complete explanation, raise your hand to tell me your partner has learned it. I'll hold you responsible for reporting accurately that your partner could explain the whole thing.

They'll ask, "What did you say? What do we have to do again?" They'll worry that they may get it wrong and be embarrassed, so you rephrase: "You're just practicing telling what we talked about. That's all. And when your partner has it learned, raise your hand to let me know. Is that clear?"

Verifying someone else's work product *against a written standard* is easier than rising to a standard themselves—hence the need for specific hard copy. You've helped them compile a complete, correct written answer, and they need only compare the other's report to it: "You left out point three," or "You got all the steps. Now let me try."

Repeat the instructions a couple of times, and they'll be confident they won't embarrass themselves. You don't put them on the spot in front of the whole class but let them do the mistake-prone, uncertain work privately with one other student to shield their self-esteem.

The first day you try this, the effort will probably succeed haltingly, but as you repeat it, transition time will drop. Once taking their own deliberate aim at mastery, kids will use time better. They will listen more carefully to what you present because they know what they'll do with it. They'll speed on to create the written summary, divide into partner pairs without hesitation, and plunge into practice.

Why? Because the end point is public success, whose energy infuses the practice leading to it. Their partner will raise their hand and say, "Rex knows it," and Rex responds "and Jason knows it too."

4. Do the Same Thing Repeatedly

To enable students to remember permanently everything they learn, you need only ask them to maintain recall of the specific chunks. A few minutes at this first thing in the day works well. Recounting previous ideas gives them confidence about what they wade into next: "I'm going to add this to what I've mastered already." You've gotten them to flying altitude. The hard part is behind them, and from here on the activity is easy—enjoying their mastery by recalling it occasionally.

When presenting new material, always compile a compact written summary, and always have them explain it to a partner until they both know it. Keep track of what they claim to master, and periodically ask them to recall it without looking.

SUMMARY

1. Expressing knowledge is usually the point of having it.
2. The activity of explaining stimulates the six inner efforts noted in chapter 3.
3. This means each student talking at length rather than listening to the teacher.
4. Instead, students usually get less than a minute apiece to talk in any class hour.

5. Students should explain whole subjects instead of random facts from them.
6. Curriculum K–12: fifty subject areas, with students explaining more about each one every year.
7. Consolidate the knowledge to carry forward with a complete hard copy of it.
8. Present something, specify priorities, partner up, and explain it back and forth till mastered.
9. Periodically ask students to recall what they know without looking.

SIX

Developing a Mental Field: What Comprehension Looks Like Inside

IDEA OF A FIELD

A mental field is where you go inside when you think about an issue significant to you. It's comprised of a host of memories, facts, assumptions, and interpretations that hang together. Because these aspects are connected, when you tug on one idea, it leads you through others that cohere, something like opening a familiar cupboard and having all its contents immediately before your gaze and available to your grasp.

For many things we do these days, we use half our attention and they turn out okay. But with a challenge before us, we think differently. If my wife says to me, "The vacuum cleaner isn't working," my attention goes to a range of associated details. My mind flashes over a place to work, tools to gather, and actions to carry out, and I *enter* the activity.

If someone asks me to do something else, I might say, "I'm busy now but should be done in X minutes." My mind is immersed in particulars that belong together and presume a certain concentration. I exclude other concerns if I'm to do it correctly, and I do it best if I *invest* in the field and don't try it while distracted. Remaining inside the field, I'm less likely to overlook key factors. My mind is able to employ reflection to select the best actions.

For students, we want them investing that way in a field of confidently mastered knowledge subject by subject—what they look at when reflecting on what they know, a body of impressions sustained by recurring attention to it. The field needs to persist without leaning on papers, books, and credits; it needs to stand on its own as a presence in the mind.

In order to think effectively about anything, we need to install the relevant details in the field and then be able freely to alter their arrange-

43

ment. People do this "advanced" activity by first gathering an array of ideas and then reasoning, analyzing, and applying them and associating them one with another.

COMPETING FIELDS

The mental field in which students open their day is their personalized version of their immediate situation. As they sit before you—perhaps laggards delaying—some are quiet, still engaged in the field they brought from home, and others chatter, reestablishing their turf with peers. Deliberate thought comprises much of it, but their assumptions about themselves and their world size up events unconsciously. Relationships adults label as distractions may be their central stream where they promote their self-image and express and manage their feelings.

A detail comes before them, and their perceptions instantly peg it. Here is the teacher, they note, who poses a task. They guess what might occur. They survey their resources and wonder if they can cope, hoping for the best. If the teacher delays or focuses on a distraction, they exchange glances and drift back to the concerns in their attention moments ago.

They may be alternately worried, self-conscious, anxious, assertive, judgmental, bored, daydreaming, or distracted. Each has already configured an internal home base, and the teacher stands before them about to attempt to alter it.

The operating energy to start with is the teacher's assertion of will over students. The latter *respond* to a request, an assignment, or a question that emerges from the teacher's field of knowledge, even when it's telling them, "Go find a topic on your own." The teacher's viewpoint dominates until it can transfer intrinsic power to the student's viewpoint.

Here we suggest entering their internal arena, establishing a beachhead for a field different from their prior one, and gradually transfer learning content into it. Since to do this we ask them to release what satisfies them now, we need a different way for them to find satisfaction within our model. If they need to talk, we can arrange for them to talk about their subjects. If they need to enhance their social image, we can arrange it through sharing and demonstrating learning. For us to direct their minds into a destination field, it needs to be potent enough to displace their current preoccupation with friends, social image, feelings, and personal issues.

What meets the eye may differ from what's happening within them. Whether or not we like it, their prior field persists because they hold onto it. Its center may be tenacious even though they appear to comply with our requests. A sign is how easily they're distracted from learning. If they continue studying despite others' attempts to divert them, an internal field claims them.

It's like pushing a car. You bring it over a rise, it starts downhill, you stop pushing, and it continues. If instead it backs toward you, it has no internal momentum. If students' minds wander when you don't direct them, their internal field doesn't grip them. Leaving the room offers a clue. Do they notice when you do so, and when you return have they ceased to study? For most students, unless academic concentration is *made* the focus, it remains on the periphery of their attention.

We needn't blame them for being undisciplined. Rather, we work with the fact that they monitor their surroundings constantly for danger and benefit. That they're with peers matters most. They notice everyone's actions within sight and hearing and assess them against their own needs so that all remain aware of each other.

The power of this need explains why teachers may find it so difficult to focus students on learning and why students drift so quickly. Everything they think and do is conditioned by the overwhelming fact of their impact on each other rather than by the mental field containing what adults assert they should know.

To seize the moment, you may say, "Please look at the board," take marker in hand, draw a diagram, and print a couple of words. In nudging their field, you assert a competing priority, reminding them that adults represent power over them and that you expect them to absorb thoughts presented. Your energy often is enough to carry them, but lesser motives play about their awareness. Will they be put on the spot later if they don't pay attention? Will they endure consequences? Will it save them time and work if they get it now? Do they need to assert their independence by distractive comments? Do they want to show off to their peers with passive-aggressive rebellion?

In the usual classroom design, unfortunately, two fields may conflict. The one containing our direction collides with their existing self-image with all its priorities and concerns for self-direction. Then we try to introduce a third. We want the field of learning itself to fascinate them and draw them into the internal structure and qualities of the subject.

We don't achieve this by chopping up their knowledge into a few answers to questions. Fascination with the field arises largely from their sense of freedom and mastery to think flexibly within it.

Typically, instead, the teacher supplies everything: the direction for the day, the subject to work on, the detail focused on, and the question eliciting the detail. The student draws on hints and props to supply a right answer presumed to verify that he or she knows the subject, continuing the error of making learning hour by hour a reaction to a teacher's help. The students never row their own boat *directly into overall comprehension of the field itself*—using fully the forward motion of their own mind based on what they securely possess already.

A reliable mental field is a clue to the presence of an education. If little of it remains when the teacher relaxes, then the teacher's ability to think has substituted for the student's instead of leading it to its own competence. Without a mental field sustaining it, students often summarily dismiss their learning when they leave school and to the end of their days remain the effect of the forces around them.

We can even set it up so that to learn they have to struggle against both us and their peers, ensuring that any idea we present won't survive. A student inclined to interest in a subject may be discouraged by an anti-intellectual peer group created by our instructional design on the one hand, or a dominative teacher making him- or herself the issue may inspire rebellion on the other. When mental fields collide, the one containing the subject matter may be reflexively dismissed as soon as adult pressure backs off.

Instead we want the knowledge field to be the student's inner axis, persisting beyond outer influences. We start it off through our instruction and then arrange peer interactions to reinforce it with reciprocity, respect for competence, shared experience of success, and good feelings. We enlist peer group influence to support their desire to learn.

HAVING A MENTAL FIELD

To have a mental field, we remember specific ideas long enough to weave their connections together. This is the "loading cargo" step. We can think freely about a subject only to the limit of ideas we retain one at a time. We achieve freedom of thought only by surrendering some freedom to discipline ourselves to the acquisition of knowledge.

Teachers' demands don't ultimately determine the effort required to learn. Students' brains dictate what it takes, a discipline much the same across the human race that I summarize as *learn, save, learn, save.*

Many recognize education's deficiency in failing to take students' thinking beyond the simple reproduction of what they learn, but advanced thinking has a price. It presumes a prior body of more basic thinking. Years back I might have said, "You don't climb the peak of a mountain without climbing the base first," but our culture has come to expect that we can start at the top—helicopters save enormous effort—and needn't push our way through the weeds and bushes. In education, in contrast to mountain climbing, we have to start in the weeds and bushes. We first need basic skills and information about the world and think higher only about what we've already at least gathered.

This is particularly clear when we distinguish an inner arena from an outer one. If you regard your education as books and papers *you can buy,* you jump to the front of any line. Suddenly you have an education—there it is on your shelf! You drop "education" on it as you pay for it. Any "base before peak," any sense of sequence, disappears. Once familiar with it, you credit yourself with being educated about it.

Even the idea of practice has no place in that picture. Each item to which we apply the word "learned" is but a single task completed. Nothing need be saved deliberately that isn't saved automatically. The transcript is the context: "I want to get my credit and do something else." Students are led to believe that their printed list of courses *authenticates* them, though based on arbitrary checkpoints that may correlate little with actual learning.

Once recognizing that practice is significant, you change arenas. You cease preoccupation with compliant activity and look closely at what you actually have in mind. You stop claiming that your bookshelf represents your knowledge and admit instead that it's only the aborted beginning of what you might have learned. If you were to narrate its actual contents, you might have scant to say—a book title here and there, a few sentences from a report or a text you carried about, or random memories of teachers and discussions.

I've noticed in talking with people whose education hasn't formed a mental field in them *that I cannot tell whether they had any given course.* They may have herded ideas through their mind, but none lingered enough to inform their conversation with me. Recall the study of the 12,000 high school students and their superficial learning of biology. People *who don't intend to think differently* as the outcome of a course don't retain its influence on their mind. Even if they achieve education's narrow purpose of certification, for its wider purpose of learning something their time was a waste.

Your students do have a mental field, of course, but it's not spontaneously about what you teach. You can initiate one to expand on further by suggesting, "Let's brainstorm everything we know about this subject already." The field's depth varies from student to student but persists by their conscious attention to it. Opening a book isn't enough. They need instead a sense of *entry*, walking into a familiar internal arena containing memories and perceptions.

Teachers short-circuit the steps of creating and reentering the mental field of a subject, I believe, because they want to be efficient. Wondering what we can discard and still obtain the same results, we remove parts from objects and watch how they function. Can we still get satisfactory education in a cheaper building? With plain desks and chairs? No carpeting? No art décor or stained-glass windows? Probably we can if we must.

But does the same subtraction apply to the influences on student minds? The short answer is, "Nope." Children's physical bodies still stand before us, and they appear to do fine. They don't dissolve even if we mistreat them, and by means of their ingrained investment in life they bounce back repeatedly despite our mistakes toward them. But we have to wonder. We're affecting an invisible resource. We may not notice that our mistakes add up like pollution creates an ocean dead zone. We take a toll on their inner life that sooner or later manifests.

From the outside, we look at *their minds, their minds, their minds.* What's happening in that closeted venue? They are so versatile, so hungry, so impressionable—so why not impressed by what we wish to teach?

This may exceed your image of your role, but I believe that you have the power to transform your classroom as it stands if you know what to ask of them. Get clear that developing a mental field through practice is simple. You do it by steadily challenging them to reproduce knowledge.

BOY WITH ONE BOOK

To rank the conditions you might enlist, note the essentials in the picture of a boy in a poor country. He barely knows how to read and write and at age twelve has no school. His father labors for a landowner who gives him a book for the boy. Since this is the only one he has, he determines to learn it, sits under a tree, and begins.

He reads a paragraph, looks up, and being hungry to master it, thinks about it. He forms a mental representation of it. For words he doesn't get, he walks home, asks his mother, and returns to reading. His objective isn't to get through the book and receive credit for it but *to delay its completion so he can savor it.* He understands, translates words into mental images, and reads on.

At a certain point, we can assume that images confuse him, presenting a fork in the road. One direction is easy that, if pursued long enough, nonetheless leads to learning. He skips the hard parts—words and ideas he doesn't understand. He reads ahead, and as he does so, understanding accumulates.

In the harder way, he *thinks about* the first paragraphs. He holds them in mind, recounts them in his imagination, and connects them as best he can before adding more. His pace is slower because he refuses to race on and appears to learn haltingly, but in fact moves rapidly because he needn't repeat anything.

Even by the end of the first day, he can say to his father and mother, "Let me tell you what I read today." He's exercised the most fundamental learning method: Learn a piece, save it, learn another, save it, integrate the two, learn another, save it, integrate the three, and so on—a cycle at the heart of learning. Without the saving step, pieces learned dissolve into a featureless heap. A few are recalled, many are smudged, and others are lost.

The boy's approach offers continuous success because he can explain what he reads. He experiences no failure, so his confidence remains high. Whatever he doesn't understand yet is just the next thing to learn—no need to label it negatively. We remove expectations, pressure, and arbitrary checkpoints and say only, "You're doing fine. Just add more," which is the central progress report students should hear from us.

For the child less intrinsically motivated, a significant person listening to him can be a support, to which a teacher might object, "Well, *my* students don't have supportive parents! They don't have a drive to learn and wouldn't read a book on their own." I'm reminded of the high school student discussing with his mother a birthday present for one of his friends. She suggests a book and he replies, "No, he has a book."

If they wouldn't read on their own, you can arrange it. Pair them up, set them to read, and ask each to explain to the other what they just read. Arrange balanced learning as described by Francis Bacon: "Reading makes a full man, writing an exact man, and conference (conversation) a ready man." Everyone needs all three skills.

The boy under a tree with a book has one more lesson for us. Curiously, he is freer yet more disciplined than most of our students. He points his attention directly into the teeth of the effort to learn the book. Notice what this looks like and compare it to how we manage students. We limit their freedom as we confine them to a single chair, tell them to stop and go here and there at set times, order them to produce this and cease that, and require their responses now and later.

Minute by minute we supplant the discipline of learning itself. Since our control of them goes to such lengths, it should at least yield greater learning. Instead, students often chafe under it, learn little, and still feel bored, aimless, and frustrated. If they receive their credit, they sigh with relief and toss the paper on the shelf alongside other proof that they are educated.

Speculating on the mental field of an eighth grade class, we can imagine them thinking comprehensively about geometry, the American Revolution, and the effect of pollution on life forms. We want them drawing on an internal field under their command that satisfies them when they reflect on it, able to tug on one end of a string of ideas and follow it to the others.

Forming it is hardest, but once possessing a field, they can seize on an aspect and move it about by writing, drawing, discussing, outlining, searching, designing, or computing: the mind sifting the field for what's actionable today. We reground learning from being reactive, superficial, and familiarized to being personally formed, substantial, and mastered as they assemble a mental field from the details we arrange for them to practice.

SUMMARY

1. A mental field is what we use inside to think in a connected way about a topic.
2. We need to install details deeply enough that we can rethink their arrangement.
3. A teacher constantly faces competing fields.
4. The field we teach has to be satisfying if students are to stay in it willingly.
5. Conversation about it reveals the presence of a mental field.
6. Without a mental field, students usually cannot talk about what they have tried to learn.
7. We develop their mental field by asking them to reproduce knowledge in larger chunks.
8. The discipline of learning is to focus on a point, grasp it, and express it.

SEVEN

Practice Saves Prior Learning: The Cycle of Deepening Mastery

Like flying an airplane, the point of learning is not to get off the ground only to land at once, but to carry a load somewhere. The take off is the big challenge. You stress the machine to raise it to cruising altitude, but then the trip is easy. Maintain forward momentum, *don't dump your cargo*, and land where you expected.

The effort of learning is similarly front-loaded and hard at first. But once you've mastered a subject, maintaining it is easy, fun, and more satisfying than constant learn-and-forget. We want to use time efficiently so that the first minute of learning is a solid step toward its permanent retention. When classroom time is used poorly, knowledge is continually repaired for some, entirely retaught for others, or never learned at all for others.

Assuming your students reach cruising altitude with their cargo, how do they save what they've grasped?

EXPANDING INTERVAL REPETITION

A familiar principle is that for efficient learning we recall the same material at increasingly longer time intervals.[16] Misunderstanding this, however, most teachers *confuse recall with review*. Review re-presents the material to the surface of the mind, while recall retrieves it from the depths of the mind, a substantial difference.

Think of your own response when you take a course and an instructor says, "We're going to review this." Most telling is that you think, "This is going to be *easy!*" though perhaps boring. It won't put you on the spot, won't tax you. Even if a teacher throws out questions, there's no downside to not remembering. Instead, you have a series of recognitions: "Knew that," "knew that," "forgot that but have it again," and so on. Passing your mind over the same ground encourages you to relink isolated pieces and reform the whole again.

Enough of it can in time lead to greater comprehension of the material. But since there's no limit to what one can review and no point at which it's certifiably complete, its variable cost-benefit discourages teachers from doing much of it except when they want enough surface knowledge for their students to face a test. *There's no point at which review reaches a specific objective.*

To define an objective, we have to turn to recall. What really sinks material into the mind is recall *without first reviewing.* A student's ability to do this, in fact, offers an objective measure of the depth of remembered material: How long since a student last looked at it can he or she still recall it perfectly? We can tally its depth according to the length of time in days since the student last looked at a hard copy. As we expand the number of days, we plot increasing depth.

Teachers appear confused about this. Since they can't tell day to day how deeply their students know something, they resort to scheduled tests. Yet knowledge temporarily useful from cramming may hold a day while we need it for months or years.

We can instead draw on the principle of expanding intervals from the very first to learn key material exactly. In brief:

1. Practice it enough that you can read a small piece, look up, and recite it accurately and completely. For gauging chunk size, aim at between three and seven novel bits—words, symbols, facts, or numbers that express the advance in students' knowledge. Usually the new are fused with the familiar in a sentence or two. Once you can tell it back error-free, even looking at it just moments before, you have a correct internal model ready for permanent mastery.

2. Turn your mind away from it for a full minute, think about something else, and then recall it without looking again at the hard copy. This secures the idea. You have it. You assigned the material to memory, turned your attention elsewhere, and memory held on.

3. From there, you need only expand the intervals, each time "without looking." If you forget a piece, return to the prior interval successfully, and then expand the intervals again.

4. Optimum intervals may vary for different material but generally go like this: After the first full minute, wait three to five minutes, then fifteen to twenty minutes, forty-five to sixty minutes, three hours or until the end of the day, and then in growing numbers of days. Material that's impacted the imagination or arises from direct experience tends to be easier to learn so that intervals expand more rapidly. At each point, it continues to be important to turn

the mind *away from the subject matter during interval time*, and then draw the material straight from unaided memory.

This method is especially valuable for perfect retention of essential formulae, sequences, outlines, and translations. In an hour students can start off three such chunks toward their expanding intervals and get difficult material on track to exact and permanent mastery.

SCHEDULED MASTERY PRACTICE TIME

Beyond mastering key knowledge with expanding intervals, a continuing challenge is the stream of new daily knowledge you'd like to bring to that level. To accomplish this systematically, students need only regular practice. First, identify the questions eliciting the knowledge you want them to retain. You might say:

> Take out a sheet of paper. Print *Final Exam* at the top. As we go through material day by day, we'll write on it every question you need to be able to answer by the end of the term. You'll use the list to practice from, so keep it handy. It will help you tell for sure exactly what you know and don't know and what you need to practice more. Keep your written answers and handouts separate in your binder.

After the material is identified, students need regular time to practice it. If you end each class with new material they've grasped, the logical time to deepen it is the first five minutes of the next class for that subject, usually the next day.

The Bracelet Aid

Assign partners systematically and post them ahead so they can immediately find each other and set to work. You expand their social relations by pairing everyone eventually with everyone else using the bracelet aid.

Write their names in a column on lined paper so they're evenly spaced. Trim the list into a long strip, bring the bottom around to the top, and tape the ends together so the names are listed evenly around the outside like a bracelet.

To assign partners, crease it between two names, secure it with a paper clip, and read off partner assignments back to back. Advance it *one name* when you want new partners. Pair the two at the ends if you have an even number of students in the class. With uneven numbers, make a triad to include the unpaired student.

Partners hand each other their list of questions and take turns asking and answering as time allows back to the beginning of the course. When they've recalled as much as they can, they open their notes and refresh their thinking on points they missed or could do better. Consider a full period, such as an hour on Friday, so they enter the weekend with a grip on new learning, especially anything complex.

Because they all have their own list, students can add to it questions from individual reports, projects, or research. Once they understand how to use mental movie (next) you can alternate it daily with working in pairs. Again, it's important to wean them from looking at the material before they answer questions. Have them instead go directly to recalling it. They check their hard copy only if they can't remember all of it.

MENTAL MOVIE

Whenever you present new material, you can ask students to close their eyes even for a minute and recount in sequence everything they remember about it. At the end of a day, use three minutes: "Start at the beginning of the day and recall everything said, everything you did, everything you learned." Let them remember rising in the morning, coming to school, and beginning their classes.

Once familiar with this, they can easily extend the material addressed: "Close your eyes now and go back to the beginning of the course and remember everything you can call up about it." Students appear to enjoy doing this. We discuss it further in *Changing Attitudes and Behavior: Practice Makes Permanent*.

TV COMMERCIAL TIME

Older students interested in expanding their mastered knowledge have a ready resource they can use on their own. For those who watch TV, an hour of it contains twenty minutes of commercials. Typically they don't watch the commercials anyway and use the time aimlessly. Instead:

1. Near where they sit, place in a box all the assignments they do, books they read, and course materials they complete.
2. When a commercial comes up, mute it and draw something randomly from the box.
3. Mentally review everything they know about it without opening it.
4. Finally, browse through it and use the remaining time to affirm and correct their memory of it from the written material. Using time they would otherwise waste, they can help maintain everything they have learned with no loss to other activities.

CLASS EXPERT

Students usually enjoy what they know well or can improve at, seldom what's left incomplete or partially understood. When they notice they enjoy their uses of mind, all their learning can piggyback on that feeling. Teaching all subjects to the point of mastery enables them to affirm their competence and give themselves a deserved pat on the back.

Class expert takes personal interest a step further. Have each student select a subject or issue about which he or she can gather information, learn it well, and answer questions. Compile a list that teachers and other students can draw on: You want to know about iguanas? George in third grade is your man. You're starting the physics of planetary rotation? Sheila in senior high is your go-to. Ants? Ikena in first grade has a rap you should hear.

Each one's expert listing notes the amount of time they can expound on their point. A kindergartner might do worms for two minutes, and a high school student chemistry of the sun for a half hour. Class experts can be called on to demonstrate their competence throughout the school or district. Spark interest in any new section of a course by having a slightly older student expound on it for a couple of minutes. He or she gets respect, and your class gets an example.

SPEAKER'S BUREAU

People tend to measure the worth of their actions by the number and significance of the people who value them. Since students are important to each other, we draw on this daily as they practice together, but to put a rocket under their motivation, enlist the community.

Let organizations, media, and talk shows invite class experts to demonstrate their knowledge. This can nudge students to choose subjects of local interest; on the coast, beaches, oceans, and fish; in the Great Plains, farming. They may live near timberlands, mountains, mining, or manufacturing or have families in the professions. And society's myriad unsolved problems invite objective analysis.

Students are likely to value knowledge more as they perceive a scrap of it taken seriously. If no one else ever refers to what teachers tell them is important, how can they believe it? Contrary experience is tough to deny. We want them to notice that society honors the substance of what they learn, that the ideas they speak have intrinsic worth.

How different this is from acknowledging their learning with a luncheon for those of a certain grade point *while saying not a word about what they know.* Implied is, "What you learn isn't important to us, but we appreciate that you worked at it." If we expect the content of their learning to matter to students, it should matter to society.

MASTERY GAME

A problem often encountered with the use of rewards is the lack of a direct correlation with increased learning, yet a gamelike atmosphere can add zest to learning. By attaching rewards to the specific and objective definition of mastery offered above, we solve that problem. Students realize that valid learning gets them valid chances to win prizes. Some might be the use of specialized audiovisual equipment, computers, and computer games; being first for desired opportunities; or dispensation from particular rules. Students might identify appropriate rewards that would spur them, or a parent group could work at this.

Use three boxes to combine prizes with mastery. In one, place a slip for each separate prize; in another, all students' names; and in the third, slips for each question they learn the answer to, ideally *The Compleat and Total Final Exam.* Daily for three minutes draw a question, give them a moment to think, and draw a name randomly. If the student knows the answer competently, he or she gets to draw randomly from the prize box, and you go on to the next student (see also note 17 in chapter 8).

SUMMARY

1. Make the first minute of learning a step toward its permanent retention.
2. Recall at expanding intervals is basic for retention.
3. Recall retrieves learning from the depths of the mind; review, from its surface.
4. Measure depth of learning by the number of days since last looking at the material that a student can still supply a perfect answer.
5. To gain perfect mastery, retain a complete answer just for a minute. Then expand the time intervals since last looking at it.
6. Schedule mastery practice weekly. Students question each other from the start of the course.
7. Pair up each eventually with all others by using the bracelet aid.
8. Have students run a mental movie of all their learning from the day, week, and entire course.
9. Older students can use TV commercial time to maintain all their learning.
10. Let each student become expert at something he or she can present to other classes.
11. Offer a student speaker's bureau to the community.
12. Link points mastered to a classroom drawing for prizes.

EIGHT

Practice Behavioral Knowledge: Knowing as the First Step to Doing

When the B-17 Flying Fortress was developed in World War II, pilots had much more to do, and designers assumed they would need intensive training. Then the pilot who had assisted the plane's development from the start, rated the best, took up an early model and crashed it by forgetting a step. Designers realized that if even he could forget something, more training wasn't going to help. They settled on a checklist. *A checklist* enabled ordinary skill to pilot the Flying Fortress.

On that theme, a growing practice is reducing deaths in hospital intensive-care units: *doctors required to use checklists.* What a comedown! Imagine. A highly educated physician with comprehensive understanding is told what to do from a *list* on a piece of paper. Yet precisely such specificity about critical details spells life or death for many patients.

MASTERY OF SPECIFICS

In contrast to these examples, notice *how vague is students' knowledge*, how inconsistently they act on it, how quickly it deteriorates, and in self-management how clueless they often are. Try to imagine them instead with the B-17, intensive-care kind of knowledge—specific, thorough, and orderly in details but comprehensive in understanding.

And yourself: Do you systematically do anything important enough to warrant the discipline of a checklist? Do your students learn anything worth the effort to get it exact, mastered, maintained, and applied?

We'd prefer that they pass tests, of course, but long before, we face their very alignment with school. They no more set foot in the door than we note habits they've got wrong. If we're mainly concerned with surface results, we may address only the behavior.

A moment's reflection, however, explains why this one is quiet and that one noisy, this one interferes and that one is helpful. They configure their behavior differently. Around friends, what do you do? Of course! You talk and play. Around others, what do you do? Of course! You criticize, blame, ridicule, tease, and fight. When you see something you want, you take it. The behavior is invariably the outcome of the idea, so if we only confront a problem after the student has done it wrong, we push only on the visible portion.

Children may back off a behavior due to our pressure on them but then repeat it. Why? We have a dog and a tail, a way of thinking and a behavior. We get a firm grip on the tail and try to wag the dog, but the tail is a wobbly handle. The behavior *follows* the idea, so we have to change the idea if we're to influence the behavior reliably. We don't just suppress the behavior but from it open a conversation about how the student thought in order to act that way.

DRIVER'S MANUAL

If *consciously learning* specific behavior seems to you too rigid or limiting, remember that any branch of adult mastery depends on givens, conditions taken for granted among people who share them. Think of auto traffic. People are more likely to drive safely if they know the rules. In any occupation, shared knowledge makes common effort possible.

Education has an elaborate set of givens. Regularities catch the eye—the physical plant, adult roles, and patterned child activity—but they don't account for variances in effectiveness.

Good and poor schools appear to do about the same things, so we search out the more subtle ones, what it means to "do school"—the instructional model, actions that sustain a learning community, how to make the students' education hum; what to do with attention, concentration, order, cooperation, discipline, teamwork, and communication. Attitudes figure in, and basic components are in play from the first hours in kindergarten. We might think of this key information as the school equivalent of a driver's manual.

A driver's manual focuses on what a driver *does*, the behaviors that comprise the minimum for participation. If new learners master at least these, they can share the road with a more sophisticated driver. The manual spells out their mental plan for the key actions.

SCHOOL MANUAL

From what I see, students appear *to carry out perfectly the plan they have in mind.* Nuances and undertones coloring adult actions haven't developed yet. Lacking complicated threads they must think through, they employ the one simple idea in their direct awareness.

To shape it, students can learn a school manual from their first hours inside the door. With a few days' effort, they can assimilate an accurate picture of the school's principles of operation, the attitudes necessary, actions to carry out, and how to manage knowledge. Their ability to answer explicit questions about these things comprises a common frame of reference, a *plan* distinct from the later *behavior* the plan governs.

Like a driver's manual helps people master the thought processes of driving before they're turned loose on the roads, we want to activate thought-forms that aid students in solving at least the difficulties we know they'll face. We first enable them just to explain the plan as an idea. Once they learn to apply a new guideline and succeed with it, they're likely to value guidelines and are more willing to learn others.

This isn't hard to arrange for most of what we want them to do, just as it's not hard to get millions of applicants past a driver's test. As students get the plan clear and master it before applying it, their later behavior flows freely. Having power over the plan increases their ownership of and interest in the results.

We revert to this level spontaneously. Let's say we lecture children for an hour about how to treat people, the value of personal space, and the necessity of respect, and they still don't get it. We then take one child aside and explain this perspective face-to-face. If even this doesn't help, what then? What we do is boil down our many threads of thought into the command for the action we want: *Keep your hands to yourself.*

Such bottom-line specificity is what makes the driver's manual work: "Do not turn the wrong way into a one-way street!" Often in classrooms vague pressures come and go, but if I negotiate a solution to a second-grade conflict, I expect to be specific: "Jason, understand that what you said hurt Jennifer's feelings. Can you apologize to her now?" I look at him respectfully and wait. Time passes. He finally collects himself and says, "I'm sorry, Jennifer."

I can also say, "Jennifer and Jason, when people hurt each others' feelings, they should respect each other, and it's a good thing to apologize," and then walk away, leaving their response up to them. While I can't plot the outcome statistically, I'm reasonably sure that the second version reduces Jason's likelihood of apologizing by at least 75 percent. The slight difference is in specificity, that the idea applies right then, and that everything else stops until it occurs. Schools often work at these behavioral guidelines with colorful posters declaring that we behave well here. While advice, discussions, admonitions, pictures, and media presentations have a place, within this gauzy picture *explicit mental plans still directly precede specific application.* Just before they act, students reach for the one they'll carry out. Here we suggest deliberately conveying clear mental plans for situations certain to occur.

MICROMODULES

We can flesh out an overall model with brief, distinct, targeted modules students learn, discuss, and master. Once we have offered a clear guideline or rubric, we check their assimilation of it and allow them to enjoy mastery of it *as a concept.* With this, they can no longer plead that they didn't know or forgot. We eliminate excuses by practice of the modules and then recognize and reinforce students as they apply them. Learning the guidelines ahead, students grasp concretely what to do before they must face the actual situation.

You may say, "We already do that." Maybe so. While your school may be among the many that commit time and resources to this issue, in most schools the manual probably sits on a shelf. *The challenge is to get the idea off the page and into the thinking that governs action.*

A new driver cautiously makes a right turn, hears a police siren, and pulls over. The officer approaches and says, "Sir, you just made a right turn the wrong way onto a one-way street." Recognizing the arrow for the one-way street had to occur at the moment the driver chose to turn. Later wouldn't work. The problem for us, like the designers of the B-17, is to get key ideas working at key moments.

To achieve this we make sure the student knows the idea comprehensively and thoroughly before having to apply it. We assume that humans operate by the plan they have in mind, that children's plans channel physical and emotional drives, that plans improve when applied by conscious choice, that we can install many brief ones enabling them to succeed quickly, and that we can enlist them to teach the plans to each other. Consider those below a template into which you can insert your own preferences.

1. Make up a wall chart with students' names down the left and nine columns spaced to the right, one for each of the eight groups of modules below and another for a cumulative total. In the boxes beside each student's name, jot and update the number of answer points for each question the student learns within the category for that column. If a question has three parts to the answer, the maximum score for that question is three.

2. Teach the modules important for your students. Either post them where everyone can see them or provide each with a handout.

Explain the meaning of the words, draw out their experience with the issue addressed, discuss the points at the depth you have time for, and adapt them to the students' age level.

3. Have them practice telling back all the steps of each module to a partner. Ask older students to explain them in their own words. To keep the modules fresh, periodically practice them back to the beginning.

4. At the end of each practice session, ask students to tell you the score for the answers their partner learned. Update their scores on the chart for any category they worked on.

5. Aim at perfect mastery of all the modules. You're welcome to photocopy those below for school use. When the class reaches your objective for them, celebrate with a special event. You can also stimulate interest with a raffle drawing in which every point of an answer a student learns and maintains earns him or her a chance in a drawing for prizes.[17] The first question on the list, for example, can earn three points.

1. Doing School

What do you do when someone helps you?

1. Say their name.
2. Say, "Thank you."
3. Think how you can help them.

What do you say when someone thanks you?

1. Say, "You're welcome."

How do you share things?

1. Take turns.
2. Or each use half of what's there.

How do you offer something to someone?

1. Don't break in if they're concentrating on something.
2. Wait until they're ready for a change.
3. Offer what you want to.
4. Smile.
5. Tell them when you want it back, if you do.

How do you borrow something?

1. Ask politely if you can borrow it.
2. If they say no, say, "Okay," and do something else.
3. If they say yes, tell when you'll return it.
4. Return it when you said you would.

How does the class start a new activity?

1. When the teacher asks for attention, stop what you're doing.
2. Focus on the teacher and bring yourself under control.
3. Listen carefully to the next instruction and do it.

How does the class move from one activity to another?

1. Continue what you're doing until it's time to go.
2. Watch for the teacher's signal.
3. At the signal, go to where you wait or line up.
4. Wait silently till the teacher signals to move.

What do you do with trash on the floor?

1. Get the broom and dustpan.
2. Sweep up the trash.
3. Throw it in the wastebasket.
4. Return the broom and dustpan to their place.

How do you introduce yourself to an adult?

1. Ask their name and remember it.
2. Say hello to them and add their name.
3. Offer to shake their hand.
4. Listen to what they say.
5. If they ask a question, answer it as best you can.
6. Ask them a question if you want to.

2. Having Friends[18]

What is the first rule for getting along with people?

1. To want the other to be happy and successful.

How do you greet friends?

1. Look at them.
2. Smile at them.
3. Talk to them.
4. Listen to them.
5. Stand near them.

What do you do with friends?

1. Invite them.
2. Wait for them.
3. Welcome them.
4. Play with them.
5. Help them.

What can you do for friends?

1. Defend them.
2. Watch what they can do.
3. Clap for them.
4. Say nice things about them.
5. Accept that they're not perfect.
6. Work out disagreements with them.

3. Creating Good Feelings

What can you say to people that gives them a good feeling?

1. Tell them how they gave you a good feeling.

What questions can you ask about a feeling now?

1. What do you feel now?
2. Did the feeling come from inside or outside?
3. What happened to make you feel that?

What questions can you ask about a feeling in the past?

1. Have you had the feeling before?
2. What happened then?
3. What else did you feel then?
4. What did you think then?

What questions can you ask about changing a feeling?

1. Have you tried to change it before?
2. How can you help change the feeling now?
3. What choices do you have?
4. How can I help?

How can you lift someone's feelings?

1. Be with them.
2. Be interested in how they form their inner world.
3. Ask them a question about the least negative thing they say.
4. Continue to do that.
5. Smile.
6. Share your own stories and experiences.
7. Focus on a positive quality in the other.
8. Tell them how they give you a good feeling.

How do you help someone else change?

1. Notice what they already do right.
2. Tell them what you notice.
3. Think of how they can apply it even more.
4. Suggest a plan for what they could do next.

4. Solving Disagreements

What do you do when someone else is upset?

1. Be calm yourself.
2. Face them.
3. Take time to pay attention to them.
4. Ask if there is a way you can help.

What do you do when you have a disagreement you can't solve?

1. Find an older person who can help you solve it.
2. Remember that the solution needs to satisfy both of you.

When you disagree with someone, what should you remember?

1. Understand how you treat them.
2. Try to understand their point of view.
3. Maintain good communications even if you have strong feelings.

How do you talk out a disagreement with someone?

1. Use a courteous tone of voice.
2. Explain how you think the other person sees it.
3. Change any part they say you don't understand.
4. Continue to rephrase until they agree that you do understand them.
5. Ask them to tell how they think you see it.
6. Agree on the part you can.

What do you do when others are fighting?

1. Listen to each one.
2. Tell back to them what you guess they want.
3. Suggest how they can both get their want satisfied.

What do you do when someone hurts you?

1. Describe to them what they did that hurt.
2. Say to them, "Please don't do that any more."
3. Release the hurt.
4. Obtain an adult's help.

How do you respond to someone else's energy?

1. See it as a strength.
2. Tell the person how you see it as a strength.
3. Suggest how you want them to use their strength toward you.

5. Handling Anger

What does being mad do to our bodies?

    1. We get sick more easily.

How does our anger affect others?

    1. They get mad too.
    2. They want to get away from us.
    3. They don't want to be our friend.
    4. They don't want to help us.

How does our anger affect problems?

    1. We don't think as well.
    2. We have more problems.
    3. It takes longer to solve problems.

Give three reasons for not being mad at others.

    1. You want to respect others.
    2. You want them to help solve problems.
    3. You want to think better yourself.

What is your direct power over your anger?

    1. You can let it drift away.

What can you do instead of being angry?

    1. Release the feeling.
    2. Find out what the problem is.
    3. Find a solution that works for everyone.

6. Learning

How do you learn something new?

    1. See it, hear it, or read it.
    2. Understand it.
    3. Remember it.
    4. Write it down.
    5. Tell it to someone else several times.
    6. Picture it in your mind.

How do you become skillful at anything?

    1. Find out what effort increases your skill.
    2. Practice the effort.

What skills help most in school?

    1. Listen well.
    2. Give others good feelings.
    3. Remember.

How do you concentrate?

1. Know what you want to accomplish.
2. Know where to focus in order to achieve it.
3. Ignore everything else.
4. Keep at it until your reach your goal.

7. Communicating

How do you have a perfect conversation?

1. Look at the person who's talking.
2. Leave a brief silence after they finish.
3. Use short messages rather than long speeches.
4. Include everyone.
5. Ask questions.
6. Connect with others' ideas.
7. Accept feelings.

What two questions do you ask as you work with others?

1. How can I help you?
2. What can I learn from you?

How do you let someone know you understand them?

1. Listen to them for a long time.
2. Summarize what they say and feel.
3. Do it so accurately that they don't need to correct you.

How do you get ready to talk to others?[19]

1. Notice others' desire to speak.
2. Feel respect and consideration.
3. Focus on the one speaking.
4. Wait till the other finishes.
5. Then share your ideas and feelings.

Give four simple rules for listening.

1. Look at the speaker.
2. Don't interrupt. Say, "Excuse me" if you do.
3. Ask the speaker to continue.
4. Leave a brief silence when the speaker ends.

How do you include everyone?

1. Invite those to talk who haven't.
2. Give equal time talking.
3. Ask questions and accept answers.
4. Use others' names.

How do you give others a good feeling?

1. Take an interest in what others say.
2. Ask about their feelings and accept them.
3. Thank people.
4. Give compliments.
5. Tell what they did that helped you.

How do you connect to what others say?

1. Remember what others say.
2. Use others' words and ideas.
3. Note similarities or differences compared to your ideas.
4. Describe what affects you.
5. Check your guesses about others' thoughts and feelings.
6. Summarize others' thoughts and feelings.
7. Talk out problems.

8. Achieving Goals

What two laws are at the foundation of our legal system?[20]

1. Do all that you agree to do.
2. Do not encroach on other persons or their property.

How do you become independent?

1. Make wise judgments on your own.
2. Make a promise to yourself in one part of your life.
3. Keep the promise.
4. Do that with more parts of your life.

How do you use your main power?

1. Notice your ability to think, feel, and do.
2. Notice that you can choose how to use your power.
3. Aim it at good goals that please you.
4. Notice any way you let others mislead you.

What are the four stages on the Progress Ladder?[21]

1. Undecideds
2. Entrants
3. Contenders
4. Winners

What are the qualities of an Undecided?

1. Waiting, hoping something will turn up.
2. Needs to watch others and draw from them.
3. Is learning to follow directions.
4. Works only when inclined to, when there's nothing else to do.
5. Easily sets aside goals when distracted by others.

6. Expects to succeed without any personal change.
7. Is absorbed in own feelings and can't give others much attention.

What are the qualities of an Entrant?

1. Wants to do better, but finds it hard to set things aside.
2. Needs coaching and encouragement but doesn't ask for it.
3. Drifts. Will practice and work only when directed to.
4. Others must plan for him or her.
5. More concerned with how others treat him or her than how he or she treats others.
6. Goals are more in the form of wishes.

What are the qualities of a Contender?

1. Periodically is enthusiastic. Can work hard but quits soon.
2. Has goals but loses track of them.
3. Not willing to work when others play. Won't make sacrifices to learn.
4. Confident in some areas.
5. Will give good feelings to those who return them.
6. Lets circumstances be stronger than his or her own choices.

What are the qualities of a Winner?

1. Knows what he or she wants and acts steadily toward it.
2. Practices good habits and skills constantly.
3. Can sacrifice recreation for study or work, and will do so while others play.
4. Can face opposition and keep going all day. Works even when tired.
5. Can feel down but gets self up again.
6. Gives others good feelings steadily and draws out others' best.
7. Habitually considerate and acceptant toward all.

Name two overarching personal goals.

1. To be *imperturbable,* so that even unexpected events don't shake your emotional balance.
2. To be *impeccable,* so that your actions are without flaw.[22]

Benefit from this learning depends on follow-up. Knowing the answers to the questions and maintaining them gives students at least the form of valuable ideas, but they have greater impact as they're applied. Reinforce them by recognizing their use—how children drew on a guideline, how it turned out, and what they learned for next time: "Yes, that's the idea. You're doing it." When the school draws on key practices at once, constructive habits can persist from the start. Students understand that ideas guide behavior.

SUMMARY

1. A checklist can help manage an array of standard, repeated details.
2. A school manual can serve as a checklist for what to do at school.
3. Students benefit from a specific plan for how to treat numerous situations.
4. We can express these plans as questions answered by specific points.
5. With practice, students can learn them perfectly.
6. Categories of plans are doing school, having friends, creating good feelings, solving disagreements, handling anger, learning, communicating, and achieving goals.

NINE

Students Talk Meaning: How to Help Students Express What's Important

VALUE OF STUDENT TALK

A personal question: *Do you believe that student talk is worth the time it takes to do it?* I ask because most teachers appear to believe instead that society's information is so much more important than students' own thoughts that they only transmit the former instead of developing the latter.

What students have to say can't compete, right? With time to talk, they waste it. They play, interrupt, pick on each other, make lame attempts to be funny, stay on the surface, march off on their own tangent, and get nowhere. Invited to develop their opinion or express a viewpoint, they're far off the mark—the more poignantly as their confidence outstrips their competence.

Those qualities, I believe, arise entirely out of the conditions we impose. *Every child has something to say that to him or her is truly important.* If we arrange for peers to give it respect and allow sufficient time for idea development, children learn to value and extend their ideas.

There's irony here. As a system, we give short shrift to students' ideas, yet for better or worse they'll use their unimportant ideas to guide their lives. So when they misbehave, we wonder, "What could they be thinking?" Hey, we never asked before, so now that there's a problem, *now* we want to find out? What should we expect? We presume children have faulty, valueless thinking and won't correct it on their own, but when they are in trouble, we pounce on them.

CHANGING THINKING

To start at a different point, how do we smart, educated grownups change our thinking? Much of it we process on our own, but when it's clear to us that we're confused, what next? Right, we talk to someone. We talk it out. And often, without the other saying a word, just by verbalizing our own tangled impressions we correct them.

Why don't children do this?

Answer: It's the conditions. They don't experience the conditions that elicit such thinking. They don't receive them spontaneously from each other and rarely from adults. Teachers typically have little confidence they can elicit voluntary, constructive, self-forming thinking in students. They don't trust students' ability to generate a worthy exchange of ideas.

Fortunately, we can do something about this. We can arrange for students to provide each other these conditions, and given time, they will take advantage of it. The following report captures a picture of this kind of learning. It challenges our assumptions about children's capacity to think, given the right conditions, but its lessons have been largely ignored by American education.

THE FOREST HILL VILLAGE STUDY

The objective of the Forest Hill Village study was to provide average children with an opportunity for free discussion to understand themselves, their peers, and the world.[23] It was founded on the belief that children free to talk about anything at all "will finally talk about everything." They will circle back to what matters most to them and use their best thinking to resolve it.

For an hour a week teachers went into classrooms to lead discussions in which students could talk about anything they wanted to. That the same approach was used for grades one through twelve marks it as fundamental. The teachers had had a full year's special training in human behavior and communications and an opportunity to work through their own emotional reactions to the work. They were asked to intervene as little as possible, listen to everything, clarify or summarize only if necessary, and make notes on the blackboard if asked. A classroom appeared thus:

> One teacher, with an incredible facial vocabulary, opened and closed
> sessions and kept the verbal traffic from snarling with nothing but a
> smile that moved like a warm beam from one child to another. Occa-
> sionally she said "Billy" as a child moved to speak, or, very gently
> "Jane?" as another seemed to want to, but needed "permission" to
> begin. In three months she said little more in a class of energy-bursting
> grade fivers.

Teachers were asked not to approve or disapprove but to allow students to correct each other and to accept them with "warmth and interest on a level with everything else." The process was "non-directive, unstructured, and group-determined." Everyone who wanted to talk got listened to.

Research was thorough. All children in the village were tested with a battery, experimentals matched with controls, and final testing postponed to a year and a half after the start. For those who retain their faith in research despite the decline effect, almost all of thirteen hypotheses were borne out "with varying degrees of statistical reliability." The few negative results were much time "wasted" in coming to a point, topics brought up and dropped, and some negative emotional expression.

On the positive side were emotional engagement, skillful and comprehensive use of analytical tools, ethical considerations voiced, and many urgent personal concerns dealt with. Three years later, in addition, the graduating grade ten group, a fifth of the total grade level, took four out of five scholarships on the basis of competitive examinations. Teachers were impressed at the lack of discipline problems, children's emotional involvement, their active participation, and the content of their discussion.

The results could be summarized as improved character. During a year of an hour a week, children brought up their thoughts and used them to cope with their world. They were able to identify and focus on what was emotionally relevant and were free to express and explore it.

Apparently two conditions mattered, *both about teachers*. They needed to have keen *awareness* of positive communications and needed to *manage* their own feelings. The first condition would lead them to reinforce the right things as their attention landed accurately on the positive element in children's attempts. Managing their own emotions would minimize reactions likely to close children down.

Worries that students would say the wrong things or be disrespectful were largely unfounded because, I believe, children tend to select their words according to the reaction they expect from listeners, both children and adults. The presence of an alert, balanced, benevolent teacher causes a certain channeling of thought.

The implication of this is that once the presence of nonreactive adults creates a safe environment for students to talk, *we let them talk*. If we aren't providing them the means to safely work out issues they themselves perceive as important, how can we convince them to learn anything they *know* up front isn't important to them?

In the past fifty years we've learned many more ways to refine communication and help students work through their attitudes. There's no reason any school couldn't benefit students with ongoing discussions.

PERFECT CONVERSATION

A few guidelines may help you get started.

Many years ago while I was running a small school, I was invited to a Sunday evening gathering of a dozen friends. One might hear one-to-one conversations, interruptions, laughter, and a few talking at length, but that particular evening, everyone talked together. A feeling of respect pervaded as participants valued each one's contribution and added to it.

The following morning I exclaimed to my students, "I was in a perfect conversation last night!" and wrote its features on the board. Everyone learned them, and I arranged small-group discussions to apply them. While the rules aid personal conversation separately, their combined effect shows up best in groups. The list is expanded from its original five to seven here.

1. *Look at the speaker.* This is the main signal of attention to another. If we do something right, having others look steadily toward us gives us permission to continue—a green light. When others turn away from us, we assume that their attention drifts, and their changing focus is a red light. So if we want to encourage others to talk, we first give them the basic signal. We make eye contact and continue to do so while they speak. Our willingness to look at others also signals our most basic attitude. People who love each other *want* to look at the other.

2. *Leave a brief silence after each one speaks.* This unobtrusive change improves the quality of a discussion significantly. Note how you feel when people interrupt you or cut you off. Not only do they not value what you say, they have made up their mind about its meaning before you get it all out, and they don't care that it's you speaking. Promoting their own idea is more important to them.

   A brief silence corrects these impressions. It accords enough significance to your idea to allow others to think about it after you finish it. It enables you to add a closing nuance and feel respected for it. Each can also enter in turn.

   In most groups some are quick to speak and others are more deliberate and may never get an opening. They don't like to cut others off, are willing to wait, and, because of their politeness or hesitance, may not draw on the setting to develop their thinking. Recurring brief silences say instead that the group wants to hear from everyone.

3. *Use short messages rather than long speeches.* Many students need encouragement to speak at all, but some are tempted to talk disproportionately. This guideline directs their attention toward efficiency of expression. It may need more emphasis for adults who

readily elaborate on ideas than for students just gaining confidence.

The rule works best paired with the prior one since a major reason people repeat themselves is that they don't feel they got their point across on the first try. Once assured that everyone listens to them, they're more likely to observe the slight discipline implied in this guideline.

4. *Include everyone.* With brief silences allowing all to participate, an effective group also thinks actively about each. The point of the discussion isn't to showcase the ideas of one but to give all a positive experience of sharing and acceptance. This rule encourages the group to notice if someone is ready to talk and hasn't yet been welcomed, and to invite them.

   Students might brainstorm the signals hinting that someone is ready to speak. They lean forward, look at the prior speaker, open their mouth, wet their lips, start a sentence, or provide audible clues.

5. *Ask questions.* A question about what someone just said invites the speaker to take another step. It shows respect for the idea, suggests equality between speaker and questioner, and implies that the views of the speaker deserve further attention. It also manifests the questioner's unselfishness and generosity since he or she turns group attention toward another.

   The question need not be ponderous or deep. It's a service simply to draw out another, show interest, and invite him or her to speak about any of a range of issues. Asking someone several questions in a row can let the speaker know we really want to consider his or her ideas.

6. *Connect to others' ideas.* Recalling what they said earlier and building on it compliments people, implies that their ideas are worth remembering, and stimulates our own thought. When we actually weigh what others say and comment on it, we connect. Students can easily learn how to summarize briefly another's contribution ("So you're saying that . . .") and then attach their own thought to it in response.

7. *Accept feelings.* Children are immersed in unseen feelings, leaving them with a unique personal burden. Malina Saval, the author of *The Secret Lives of Boys*, found a common thread among the many she followed for two years. It was a feeling of isolation, not being understood; that adults spoke *to* them rather than *with* them.[24] As best I can tell, few are treated to others' skills in communicating that could help them examine and resolve their feelings.

Shortly after I introduced the guidelines to my students, snow fell that was perfect for snowballs. When they went out for recess, a snowball fight erupted, and as they returned, I noted tearful faces. Some accused others of ganging up on them, an issue ideal for trying perfect conversation. With everyone watching that others followed the rules, a superb discussion evolved. Those who'd been unfair to others apologized, and the group devised guidelines for snowball fights that changed their behavior later.

The rules are easy to apply because they alter students' habits only slightly yet with a disproportionately positive effect. Looking at the speaker more than they would otherwise meets needs for attention. Everyone is more likely to feel that "others are listening to me." A few seconds' pause after others speak alters their common experience of being cut off, enabling them to sense respect for their contribution. Being asked a question instead of contradicted seems like another's interest in their idea. A focus on including everyone counteracts their customary deference to dominant students, who now give others space, and welcomes the reticent.

Hand raising ceases as the vehicle for designating the speaker. Schools overusing it discount students' capability and prepare them poorly. Adult society expects a different skill set—first *noticing* others, then listening, then a timely and appropriate response, and then developing ideas in common.

TEACH THE RULES

You can teach these rules easily with classes from second grade up starting in groups of three for eight to ten minutes at a time. With second and third grade, use just rules 1, 2, and 4 at first on any topic they want to talk about. After a few minutes, ask them to raise their hands if they're applying rule 1, then rule 2, then rule 4. Their reports should align with your observation.

Repeating the experience on successive days, gradually incorporate all the rules. Allow them as a class to brainstorm and choose topics, then memorize all the rules so they can apply them easily. Show them how: Read over a rule, look up, repeat it until they know it "cold"; then do two at a time and so on until they know them all. Assign them in pairs to "tell the whole list back to your partner without looking." Post their scores on a chart, the seven points earning a score of seven. To help them assimilate the set:

1. Students learn and remember the seven steps. They might add one per day or take the list in two pieces until they can tell it all back to a partner.
2. Assign them in groups of three to use the guidelines on topics you propose. After a teacher presented the *Odyssey* in some detail, her

third-grade class was ready to use the guidelines to discuss the values and lessons in it by themselves.

3. Propose that they pick one skill to practice and observe its effect. At first, for instance, in place of their anxiousness to express their own ideas, they might observe how the discussion improves as they ask questions of others or connect to their ideas.
4. Drift among the groups as they talk so that later you can point out skills they used. Ask them to give each other feedback on how they applied the rules.
5. Ask them to stand and tell the class how well they believe their group did.
6. Expand the size of the groups. Fours and fives require more self-discipline than threes in including others, asking questions, and not interrupting.
7. When they're competent with the guidelines, try a whole-class discussion about a topic of interest.
8. Some classes like to know that they "used the skills perfectly." You can time them for how long they do this and keep track of this score for successive discussions.
9. Older classes might share how a discussion by these guidelines compares to others they've experienced.

We assimilate ideas by installing them in our mental apparatus. We gain an impression and then describe it in words, reeling knowledge into our brain by the hooks it depends on—words. Impressions are like hot air balloons that want to rise up and away, but ropes of words attach to the basket carrying us with them. For better or worse, students run their lives by the words they speak to themselves.

SUMMARY

1. Many teachers don't believe student talk is worth the time it takes to do it.
2. Children have things to talk out that are very important to them.
3. They are rarely granted the conditions in school allowing them to do so.
4. The Forest Hill Village study demonstrated the influence of allowing children to talk regularly about subjects they chose.
5. Teachers need to understand positive communications and manage their own feelings.
6. For perfect conversation, students look at the speaker, leave a brief silence after each speaks, use short messages, include everyone, connect to others' ideas, and accept feelings.
7. Students learn and apply the rules easily.

TEN

Practice on Substantial Topics: Weigh Fundamental Issues

Once we can arrange a productive discussion and students realize that they can absorb and apply ideas, what can they talk about?

Substantial topics may directly influence their personal success and contribution to society. Explain to them the idea of working on themselves, getting better at the processes of living—that everyone has limitations, choices lead to better or worse outcomes, and all their lives they'll choose what to emphasize. You might brainstorm physical, mental, and social issues they want to know about, prioritize each list, and work down it.

THE INTERVIEW

Prepare students for a stimulating, relevant discussion by asking one to interview others privately with a single pointed question. Then discuss together the answers collected, which remain anonymous. Rotate the interviewer role. Topics should relate to their direct experience:

- What would you do if you found something valuable that didn't belong to you?
- What would you do if a friend of yours was being ridiculed behind his back?
- What would you do if you knew someone was cheating on tests?
- What would you do if you were bullied with words?
- What would you do if you were bullied physically?
- What would you do if your best friend wanted you to do something your parents forbade?

- What would you do if you could get on a school team but had to work a lot harder?
- What would you do if telling the truth meant a friend would get into trouble?
- How do you act differently toward two kinds of people—those with whom you get along well and those with whom you get along poorly?

Identify their beliefs about themselves and the world, sort the functional from the dysfunctional, and talk them out. Do they tune people out, avoid their neighbors, cut corners, lie in their own defense, steal when no one is looking, blame others, or label them? What would they choose instead?

Immersed in personal feelings as they are, students need to realize eventually that their inappropriate emotions spring from misformed ideas. Their developmental task is to choose principles that enable them and their social order to thrive. Share with them from your own life how ideas of people important to you affected you and how a single thought can generate a lifetime of application for good or ill. As they meet new situations, from their contact with you students should be able to call up worthy ideas and remember how to use them.

ONE-TO-ONE DISCUSSION

To pursue this theme with a student one-to-one, first establish basic acceptance by greetings, brief comments, and feedback on positive qualities you notice in them. Make it easy to work on an idea together. Then observe and listen carefully enough to pinpoint a change in thinking that could help the student.

Maybe it's already obvious to you, but if a child has recurring difficulty, you may need to draw out the change patiently and express it the way they see it. Write it down for them and edit it so they agree it's accurate. Get their agreement that the idea is important and that they'll try to remember and apply it when they need it. Then daily ask them how it went—did they remember to use it? Feedback from other teachers and students can help mark their success. Following are some ideas I've worked on with students this way.

- "I don't have to get mad to solve this problem."
- "I don't have to push back against teachers."
- "I can choose to be calm."
- "I can give others a turn."
- "The teacher is my friend even when he's not right there."
- "I can be good even if others aren't."
- "I can practice getting along with unpleasant people."

- "When things are hard, I learn something about myself."
- "Others don't have to like me, but I can earn their respect."
- "I can use lots of ways to be happy."

Your follow-up needs to be thoughtful and on target, but with even a few seconds contact you can make a difference. If you ask, "How's it going?," and the students answer "Great," you need to know the reality from observation. You may need to check in with them specifically:

"Remember the idea we're working on?"

"Yes." They tell you what it is.

"Have you tried it out since Tuesday?"

"Uhhh, yeah, once."

"How did it turn out?"

"It went okay. Seemed like it worked."

Many respond well to using a scale on which they rate themselves. Ask them, "On a one-to-ten scale, where would you rate your use of the idea?" Keep their answer in mind and ask again a few days later.

Students appear to enjoy tracking their progress. My first attempt at this was trying to help a fourth grader control his incessant talking. He carried a clipboard everywhere, gave himself a rating every fifteen minutes, and changed within a few days. I've used self-checking to help students manage anxious feelings, talking, attention to the teacher, concentration, choosing happy feelings, not crying, and positive feelings toward others.

A DAILY CLUE

From upper elementary on, students can benefit from a daily clue to think about, a simple idea that helps them manage their lives. To embed it in their thinking, you might (1) present a principle such as those below and others that interest you, (2) briefly explain how it can affect their lives, (3) draw out their comments about it in small-group or whole-class discussion, and (4) point out to them later how you see them apply it.

If you're tempted to defer such discussions to a high school social studies class, remember that children form their basic stance to life very early. An idea arriving as a late appendage to thinking already well established is less likely to influence them.[25]

Two basic principles, for instance, might transform a school. In *Whatever Happened to Justice?* Richard Maybury sums up centuries of common law in two statements: (1) Do all you agree to do, and (2) do not encroach on other persons or their property.[26] Think how different schools would be if students grasped these from the time they arrived.

Do All You Agree to Do

They could be trusted out of our sight. You want to go to the bathroom and you'll come right back? Okay, go. You want to do research in the library? Go. You want to work with a friend on a learning project? Do it. You're tired and need to walk around outside to refresh yourself? Go ahead. You need to borrow something and will return it when you're done? Of course. You say you'll be back in seven minutes? I'm confident you will, so go. And you'll finish this report by tomorrow? Good, I'll look for it then. Once agreeing to it, they'd apply themselves to learning outside our direct oversight.

Making agreements they keep builds character. By following through with them day by day, children develop trustworthiness. If no one ever trusts them enough to make an agreement they later keep, why should they try? Expecting people to be reliable opens them to realizing, "We're trustworthy!" If the few they know well are like that, they comprise a social group that operates by a transforming norm.

They come to understand that trustworthy people exist, that they can work together in groups and fulfill their agreements, and that believing this doesn't require them to give miscreants the keys to the vault. They learn to identify those who don't keep their word, but with those who do they develop a more advanced society.

Do Not Encroach on Other Persons or Their Property

With this understood, most of students' behavioral problems would disappear. You left your pack on the steps? It's been turned in already. You dropped your favorite pen? We'll let everyone know, and I'm sure you'll get it back. Someone nearby wants to study? You'll mute your voice once you understand. You're getting physical with others in ways they don't like? That's what we mean by encroaching.

Students wouldn't intrude into others' space or push their way into a line, wouldn't seize others' share of goodies offered. Physical objects and belongings are safe where placed, staff need not continually lock and unlock equipment, lost things are returned, and information about people is regarded as their possession. What is said and done toward others expresses respect for them.

The two principles also help students understand society. Labor, commerce, education, and caretaking depend on the first. Nothing works unless people carry out what they agree to. Our physical safety and security, and our ownership and use of our possessions, require the second. Would students like to start using the principles at school? Could they envision a society in which neither of the principles held true, and how they would stay alive?

On the basis that their choices reflect their understanding of the world, we take misbehavior not as a character flaw but as insufficient learning. We haven't steered this child's mind into a productive channel: "Ah, you don't quite have that yet. Let's go back to our discussion about the second basic law."

WHAT IS TRUE, CERTAIN, AND KIND?

Even asking this implies an ethical interest some adults lack, and the question doesn't imply that we always know the answer. The point instead is that trying to find out helps straighten out our actions and prepare students for a positive society. Often they don't notice whether they're being true, realistic, and kind but instead immerse themselves in unwarranted opinions and critical judgments. Reality isn't their concern but only what they can assert. They don't bring their ideas before a common bar of constructive behavior. Even from a well-functioning home or dysfunctional peer group they may pick up dismaying ideas about how to handle feelings like anger, frustration, boredom, blame, helplessness, loneliness, and hurt that transfer to school in comments like,

- "The teacher is a dumbass."
- "Don't rat on anyone."
- "My life is down the tube."
- "Stay away from me!"
- "Everybody steals. Stealing is just part of life."
- "Don't let anyone know what you're really thinking or they'll use it against you."
- "My life is a bummer."
- "Why bother?"
- "I don't talk to girls *and that's permanent.*"
- "Put on a good act and it may get you somewhere."
- "It doesn't matter what you know."
- "Just get through it."
- "Nothing is worth anything."

We help students question their thoughts by asking explicitly: *Is it true? Is it certain? Is it kind?* We teach them by inviting them to assess the quality of their thought and then to apply the criteria more broadly to social affairs, public issues, and the politics of regions, states, and nations.

DO NOT LEAVE THE KEY STEP TO CHANCE

This idea has aided me on countless occasions. Typically when an experience doesn't go as I'd hoped, I look back and discover, once again, a key step I left to chance.

My son and daughter visited me once with the latter's three-month-old son. As we prepared for a car trip, I heard my son, as a good uncle, ask my daughter. "Do you have the sunscreen? Do you have the umbrella? Do you have the extra diapers?"

When I called his attention to this, he said to me firmly, "Do not leave the key step to chance!" He leads kayak excursions into inhospitable conditions along the coast of Antarctica and draws on the motto at every morning's checkout. Unless reminded, he found, his clients typically forgot something they would need away from the mother ship.

We apply this idea at school by providing students an orderly way to account for crucial details. Then, from kindergarten on, we reinforce this way of thinking:

- "Everyone have your pencil ready. You need to have them sharpened and know where they are. Those are the key steps."
- "You forgot your map at home? How can you make sure you remember next time?"
- "You didn't have time to complete the assignment Sunday night? I guess you left that to chance, instead of saving enough time to get it done."
- "You thought your partner would do that part of the project? You didn't check with her and left that to chance."

Early in their academic career, students' world is soft. Mistakes don't matter permanently, and everything can simply be improved. Endings taper off, and no point of accountability holds. Later, deadlines do matter, key steps await, and students can treat them carelessly or diligently. To help them prepare, we solidify details. We help them direct their attention to produce timely results under constraints, but not with artificial pressure, threat, or personal force. Instead we want them using their foresight to ensure the next goal opening seamlessly and consciously upon completion of this one, their focus of effort sustained moment to moment.

DESIRE GOOD FOR ALL

Students too often think in terms of conflict. They may not realize that they're not required to attack some and affirm others, nor that a basic positive intent heals many disputes. No matter how difficult our situation or what others do to us or around us, we define ourselves first by what we want. Washington, Lincoln, Roosevelt, and the founders of our nation wanted good for others. People who stand out in a community are respected as others recognize that they want good for all and work toward it.

When we meet others, typically our first concern, whether or not we are aware of it, is whether *we ourselves are safe.* Are *we* safe in the presence of *their* intent? Do they want good for us, are they neutral to our well-being, or do they actively work against us? Do we interpret their disagreement with us as a threat? Should we be on the defense, ready to retaliate?

If we can manage to switch positions mentally and put ourselves in their shoes, *we know what they're thinking and what their need is.* From their viewpoint, they're wondering if *they're safe with us.* We meet their need by our decision to be a source of good for them and for all. This is the basis of trust—knowing that others will look out for us, that we can rely on them to "have our back."

When you meet others in any situation, bring with you the simple will that you'll do nothing to injure them and will benefit them as best you can. Just from this, doors will open and welcome you for your entire life. If you look out only for yourself, others will figure you out, and your life will be poorer for it. Before you ever open your mouth or do anything, notice what you *want,* what you aim at. For students to practice this in school they need only *intend others' good feeling.*

Maybe you've seen the TV commercial for the Special Olympics in which a line of children run a dash. When one falls down, they all stop, go back, pick him up, and hold hands as they complete the race. Winning for them is less important than "Take care of each other."

Easy to overlook is that *these Special Olympics children know that without being told.* Is the message so simple that only children with minds close to the basics can grasp it? That adults driven by competitiveness, ambition, and pride forget quickly that "Take care of each other" comes first?

Students may understand this vaguely as they behave a little better, are treated better in return, then feel better, and finally grasp cause and effect. Most, however, are either unaware of or unconcerned about the impact of what they do. They like their friends and discount others, and believe that this is correct.

I've explained this idea to students of all ages and they typically don't grasp it. It's evidently so contrary to their usual thinking that they drop it into a niche like an abstract principle of physics. Their picture of the world may remain willfully ungenerous and uncaring, captured by a mind-set that needs sympathetic feedback to correct. They need peers and adults around them who are alert to how the principle works and able to discuss how experience changes with it. They surrender their self-centered and irresponsible attitudes by careful feedback and discussion that help them weave together a new understanding.

WHEN TO EXPRESS FEELINGS

In practice the human brain tends to simplify even complex feelings into a yes/no question: Should I run with what this feeling urges, or check it? The question recurs constantly, and school may be the only place many will ever hear it examined.

Teachers convey their own stance by example: how they maintain their own balance, restrain their reactions with better thinking, remain aware of the effects of their actions on others, and interpret their feelings in light of the situation. Once teachers have taken care of themselves, they may reach students by mirroring what the student manifests and then moving to a constructive step:

- "So you're feeling __about__."
- "So you kept doing that until she got upset?"
- "Could we work out something else to do with that feeling?"
- "What do you think was the other person's point of view?"
- "Could we find out how he sees this?"

We want to alter the instructions they give themselves about how to handle a feeling. At first they just defer expressing it until they can turn it positive. Most need a better grasp of how to do this. They're needlessly upset over others' natural limitations, mistakes, words, or innocent actions, and they explode over trifles, make "mountains out of molehills," and take their feeling as the dominant reality.

Their success in society will depend at least partly on letting go of feelings that distort their understanding. They need to know that regardless of whether their feeling is happy or unhappy, pleasant or unpleasant, it's part of their connection to others *and they need to clean it up.* Understanding how, when, and why to let out their feelings deserves their ongoing thought.

THE MEANING OF FEELINGS

When I was running my small school, a bright boy well along in high school came to me. His relationships with practically everyone were difficult, and others saw him as volatile and unpredictable. I handed him a page listing 120 common feelings and asked him to mark those he wanted to work on. He drew a heavy circle around them all, telling me essentially, "My problem is way beyond handling a few feelings. I can't manage the entire zone."

The largest single force behind children's behavior is *the meaning they assign to their feeling.* We can influence this by letting them talk about it and understand it differently. If we don't, but leave their negative feeling intact and require only that they suppress it, we may fail to alter the pattern. And if their secret thinking remains negative inside the shelter of the classroom, what can we expect of them away from it with controls removed?

For a weekly discussion about managing feelings, brainstorm with students a list of the feelings they've felt or heard of. For kindergartners, we can start with *happy* and *sad* and work up from there. More options on this appear in *Changing Attitudes and Behavior: Practice Makes Permanent*. Older classes might be able to vote on the feelings they most want to talk about, or you can choose one.

About each feeling, (1) have a student find a definition of it and (2) have the class speculate on how it would affect someone's experience in general. Then (3) they share their own experiences with the feeling, and go deeper into (4) its sources, (5) ways people handle it or act on it, and (6) the outcomes of each way.

Typically adults tell students the meaning they think a child *should* attach to his or her experience, and sometimes it works: You should apologize, you should say "thank you," you should be glad you have a roof over your head, you should feel privileged even to be here.

But if students don't feel apologetic, thankful, glad, or privileged on our command—if at that point they can't or don't redirect their feelings— they may conclude that (1) adults don't respect or understand what they feel so they separate themselves from us; (2) they distrust their feelings or assume they're guilty for not having the "right" feeling; (3) they exclude us from their problem-solving process, believing that we'll press our ideas on them rather than work with theirs; and (4) they decide not to reveal to us what they truly experience within.

A better course is for students and teachers together to examine feelings from multiple perspectives and realize that they can choose the meaning they assign to their experience.

ENJOY SELF-DISCIPLINE

A thought from Aldous Huxley adorns a school archway: "Successful people make themselves do the thing that has to be done, when it has to be done, whether they like it or not." A businessman I know offers this to his organization: "Achievers make a habit of doing what average folks are not willing to do." Self-discipline is a basic harbinger of life success.[27]

It becomes more palatable as people redefine *liking*. They decide to like not just the outcomes of achievement but even the stresses of the process itself. They reinterpret conditions that pull others down. A Marine training officer noted on a TV interview one day that the Marines preferred recruits eighteen to twenty years old for their demanding program because "you can make them believe they enjoy it."

Charles Kettering, an engineering genius who helped General Motors become a great company, had a saying: "Problems are the price of progress. Don't bring me anything but trouble. *Good news weakens me.*" It pleased him to grapple with unmanaged conditions and bring them under control.

A major life lesson is taking pleasure in drawing on oneself to confront difficulty and to regard one's own feelings as just a condition to handle. Many undergo tremendous stresses gladly for the sake of their occupation or sport, steadily subjecting moods, attitudes, likes, dislikes, preferences, and touchiness to the laser beam of conscious thought.

We want more than compelling students to learn in the face of negative feelings, overriding their own views because we require them to. We want them instead *to see through* what they object to and find a higher perspective.

If they succeed only at suppressing emotion, it can impair their judgment. We can create stress, sap energy, and make learning distasteful, setting them up for marital and occupational disaster. Emotion denied tends to sabotage success. We instead want them to notice their feelings, learn what they have to teach, and guide them constructively.

CREATE RAPPORT

I suggested this clue to students from observing how isolated they often are and how easily this generates conflict.

Our mind does an important piece of work for us automatically. It decides whether we're safe with others and can relate to them. While we may decide this consciously, part occurs spontaneously and, if not under our control, can give us poor direction. It can tell us to stay away from people who are good for us and seek out others bad for us.

To weigh such issues, our mind makes a simple calculation: *Do we match the other person?*[28] It instinctively regards similarities as good and differences as bad, and takes account of details minor and major. A big one is the sound of our voice. Compare it to theirs by its pitch, abruptness, tone, and speed. Do our words match the kind they use? When someone enters a group and speaks even a single word alien to it, everyone notices and thinks, "He's from the outside."

Clothing can separate people. We tend to put on what we sense is accepted by those we'll join, and the mind instantly reads body position, gestures, and speed of movement. Those who move deliberately may feel uncomfortable around those who are agitated, constantly in motion. Eye contact and customary greetings have an effect. Do we greet others the way they greet us? To connect with someone, first match them in all the ways you can till you feel comfortable in each other's presence. Then move toward your mutual interest.

TEMPER ASSERTIVENESS

Some students assume that the way to succeed is to dominate others by shouting louder, pushing, or bullying, but even subtle clues matter.

Many years ago, a program to find jobs for African American teenage boys ran into a problem. Those hired were fired quickly, and employers couldn't give a good reason. They'd say, "I just didn't feel comfortable around him."

To understand why, a cameraman filmed an interaction between a teenager and his boss in ultra slow motion and discovered a simple thing. When people feel safe, they blink readily, but *the teenager would not blink first*—a posture of defiance, refusing to be vulnerable. Small, unconscious cues can separate us.

A friend of mine exemplified a contrasting view. He began working for the post office decades back as a letter carrier and retired as postmaster of a city system. When I asked him how he did it, he said that once a month he'd take his paycheck to his boss, put it on the desk, and say, "Now that's good money and I expect to earn more of it. And I want to know if you have any complaints, corrections, or commands for me."

"He's really easy to work with," his bosses would think, and when a position opened, he'd get the nod.

The point escapes many. *Assert what's valued.* Use your energy in a way that will be rewarded. If you try out for a team and then tell the coach he's an idiot, what happens? Even a good player is cut because such behavior isn't valued. People largely keep their jobs by understanding what the boss wants and giving it to him. Understand what's valued and put your energy into that. Fighting the system is a waste. If you know what you want to do, find a system that rewards it and join that one.

RUN YOUR LIFE BY IDEAS

Students may be opinionated and reactive, but if they once understand how, they can consciously apply good ideas to run their lives. Idea is the only antidote to tendency. Human nature has built-in tendencies to run all experience. Drop us anywhere and an innate inclination arises to take care of it; when all is lost, fleeing.

The problem is that a tendency may be dumb. We may desire what's bad for us and flee what's good. We may ruin what we need to build and invest in what we need to relinquish. All of us can refine our ideas so they improve on our tendencies. That's growing up. That's the meaning of education, that better ideas should run our lives.

So about everything they do, encourage students to ask themselves, *Is this my tendency or my better idea?* Is this the way I am due to unthinking inclinations, habits formed by age three now writ large? Am I running a teenage life based on ideas picked up when I was two?

You might explain to your students: Part of your development is eventually to separate yourself from adults and form the pattern of your adult life. There's no escape from doing this, so that the ideas you choose really matter. Think how you define yourself: "I hang back," or "I push to the front," or "I demand respect," or "I'm okay being lazy," or "I want to learn as much as I can," or "I want to be able to deal with people masterfully."

Pick your best idea to follow instead of your tendency. You'll rapidly become more skillful and master your life.

EVERYBODY MAKES MISTAKES

From the time we're born, we're one mistake after another. We cry, mess, and keep people awake. Before long we grab, push, break, dismantle, scream, and disobey. By the time we're three, we know one thing for sure: *Our mistakes displease others.* If they're not savvy, others might convince us that we ourselves are one big mistake, even when we haven't a clue what we do wrong.

Large numbers of students reach school already touchy about their mistakes, but teachers may daily drive them deeper. Feeling vulnerable themselves, students may then criticize others and even adopt this as an identity. "This is the way I am," negative myself and pushing bad feelings on others. Shortly, the sector of the adult world preoccupied with "Who's to blame?" welcomes them as new members.

Time spent this way is usually a waste, making us less intelligent. Negative feelings deprive our brain of the free attention with which to perceive the world accurately and understand it.[29]

We need a different angle on mistakes to start with: *They have a natural role in human activity.* Anytime we enter the unknown, we're likely to encounter them. We try something, it doesn't quite work, we learn, and we correct it—mistakes, but learning. Edison famously claimed 10,000 failures before finding the filament for the electric light bulb.

We constantly test the limits of our ability, and at this edge all of us make mistakes. No mistakes equals no edges pushed, and as we apply ideas that aren't certain and true, we come up wrong. We may dislike a person, activity, or situation and can either prune error away from our feeling or invest in it as our interpretation of the world.

So stop assuming mistakes are a mark against you, and presume instead that there's something before you to learn. Stop blaming yourself, stop blaming others, and forgive innate human limitations. Once you get that straight, you're ready to absorb any experience for the learning it offers and immediately correct your path. You progress into the unknown, improving your steps whenever you discern a better way. Grant others the same privilege, and support them as they try to do that.

Feelings commonly lead us into mistakes. We jump to impulsive conclusions that are only a guess, then think it's safer to defend them than correct them. Consistent with our past judgment, we're embarrassed to admit a mistake, double down on it, and don't acknowledge the error. Because we select as friends people who agree with us, they reinforce our errors, leading us to add their mistakes to our own because we don't screen falsehood from our collective ideas.

MASTER THE NEGATIVE

Upon experiencing negative circumstances, what do you do with them? A common response is complaining. We may blame others, blame ourselves, blame the world, and protest the fact that everything is impermanent. *We tribulate.*

Preoccupied with negatives the world appears to hurl against us, we can forget to guide our own effort deliberately. We master the negative only by understanding where to apply effort proactively and then doing it steadily. If you say, "I've mastered the art of lying around doing nothing," no one gets excited. Humans instead are designed to exert effort and take pleasure in the results. In countless ways we expend our energy and earn others' respect—raise children, repair power lines, earn a paycheck, pitch in the major leagues, or discipline ourselves to be at work on time.

To succeed, in other words, we treat the negative differently. We home in on it and draw benefit from it, which doesn't occur accidentally or just from growing up. We instead *master negative conditions.* A useful angle on this was presented by Carlos Castaneda, who wrote several books about the teachings of a Yaqui wise man named Don Juan.

He explains to Carlos that people's biggest problem is self-importance and that a good way to overcome it is to use a "petty tyrant," someone who has power to make your life unpleasant or even torment you. Opportunity arises because the petty tyrant forces you to face your weaknesses, driving you to balance and correct them.[30]

A strict or even abrasive parent or teacher can fill this role, as well as coworkers and acquaintances. In the teeth of whatever others do, *we make our actions impeccable, without flaw,* and under the most trying conditions keep our emotions joyful.

So if our experience calls up irritation or defiance, we seize the moment and return to calm self-mastery and self-discipline. If our anxiousness is called up, we master it and stay balanced. If confusion, conflicting values, and dumb thinking are called up, we bring order to them. If a

petty tyrant pushes us, criticizes us, or even condemns us, we listen carefully and learn—remaining balanced and happy.

And even if we fear for our lives, we face it with steady thought and
correct action and come through it with self-mastery intact. Don Juan
described how a tormenter plotted ways to kill him but died himself as a
result, an experience Don Juan believed transformed his life.

You set this mastery in motion by recognizing the presence of negative conditions that could upset or threaten you. Then you notice the
opportunity to extend your self-mastery ("Oh boy! A chance to grow!").
You reverse your automatic response and turn instead to the one that
restores self-mastery. The more challenging the conditions under which
you can do this, the faster you change.

ON BEING CENTER OF THE WORLD

Few students grasp how tiny is the capsule of familiarity that confines
their world. Our mind isn't constituted even to realize how incomplete is
our knowledge. We fail to notice that we're not the center of everything
because our minds warp our picture. When we look out at buildings and
sky and people, we know at the level of concrete reality that we see what
others do, but what's hidden is that each mind builds out from itself as
center. Mark Twain noted, "There are an infinite number of axes to the
world, one through every village and hamlet."

Each of us started to create our world as infants—the faces of people
close around us and of chairs and tables and beds—a tight little circle. It
expanded as we began to move under our own power. We go out and
back and collect new images into a version of the world that could be
quite different from another's. Thought by thought we build it and have
only our own to work with. We assume that that's the way the world is,
that's how reality is.

To grasp that it's truly different than how we first understood it can
be a shock. I distinctly recall a moment when I was about four years old
and discovered that my father was not God. Before that, everything he
did appeared to work perfectly and then, to my surprise, he made a
mistake.

We don't have room in our tiny brain for all the takes on reality
present in the human race. Every dog will not bite me, my father is not
omnipotent, and we have to work consciously to bring proportion to our
self-centered concept of the universe.

SUMMARY

1. Have a student interview others about how they would behave in a specific situation.
2. Have one-to-one discussions with students about key ideas that apply to their lives.
3. Offer them a daily clue to discuss in depth together.
4. The basic laws: Do all you agree to do, don't encroach on other persons or their property.
5. Topics for balance: Seek what's true, certain, and kind; temper assertiveness, weigh when to express feelings, and their meaning; create rapport.
6. Topics on effort: Don't leave the key step to chance, enjoy self-discipline, master the negative.
7. Topics for perspective: Desire good for all, run your life by ideas, everybody makes mistakes, and on being center of the world.

ELEVEN

Score Results Objectively: How Scoring Can Energize Learning

Humans love to account for effort they expend. This apparently instinctive desire drives the use of scoring—regularized measurement of the results of effort. It not only makes games and sports possible, but business and industry couldn't function without it. To achieve a complex purpose, we must distinguish reliably between conditions that lead toward and away from it, and numbers can help us do that.

Because society presumes that numerical ratings compare instances of value, children arrive at school already trained to think in terms of cost and benefit, effort and reward. Schools pick up the theme, counting and rating students' effort from morning till night.

A MOTIVATING SCORE

But of the dozens of things we might count, some deter learning. Why don't we, for instance, count up all the mistakes students make and post them? *Wouldn't we find a student with fifty mistakes listed to be more motivated than one with just ten mistakes listed?* Why don't we test them on knowledge they were never taught and then tell them they're deficient? If we try hard enough, we can scrutinize and measure them in a manner that neutralizes any natural interest they have in learning.

Several factors help distinguish a motivating score from a disheartening one:

1. Who benefits from the score? If someone from outside the classroom wants to exert leverage over the activity within it, teachers and students have more reason to subvert it than to invest in it. On

the other hand, when a group functions as a team to improve their score on an outcome everyone values, all are spurred to the effort to achieve it. Typically, perceptions of benefit vary wildly. Students may not recognize any gain for themselves in the tides of adult pressure over their test outcomes.

2. Do we rely on relative judgment rather than objective effort? A teacher or even a whole state may rate the same work far differently than another. Selecting between measures that objectively report learning versus apply personal opinion, we usually prefer the first. Personal judgments can be vital communication between teacher and student but stand apart from objective measures.

3. Measures causally remote from sustained learning distort the picture. Presence in class is a misleading indicator since one student might be asleep while another works hard. A student handing in assignments on time may really understand how to game the system. If obedience is what you want, that's what you should report: "This is a compliant child who will reliably do what you ask."

   Mastery of content is another issue. Some children will learn what's needed but are innately wired to follow their own rhythms. Our system should be versatile enough to report such characteristics fairly. We do not want to be the one who drives a future Albert Einstein to give up freshman math.

4. A score has more value offered immediately after an effort. Upon exerting ourselves, we step back and consider what we've done. We're cheered and spurred if an objective measure says to us at once, "Yes! 8 out of 10!"

5. A score is more helpful when students actively claim the result. Scoring what they don't care about motivates them less, though this influence is highly susceptible to how it's managed. The effort scored should be significant because it leads to a purpose the student genuinely wants, aside from pleasing adults. As ownership and personal interest increase, the effort matters more and hence knowing how well one is doing at it.

6. We shouldn't disengage score from energy expended. Fattening students' transcript with freebies that don't reflect what they tried to do dilutes its value. If their actual effort isn't the focus, they conclude that the whole system is specious and turn instead to activities outside school to establish their worth.

We don't want to disengage score from outcomes important to them, nor delay it, nor run it through nonobjective, control-based, bureaucratic, and politically warped criteria. We don't want to find ourselves in truth measuring how well we control students. Scores should correlate with how their effort results in successful learning.

Measurement informs management. Different levels of specificity imply different concepts of education. Some teachers need little of it. They look at their class, squint a little, and think, "He's doing great, he's fine, she's okay, worried about him—A, B, C, and D." Specific measures aren't valued because they don't influence instruction. Other schools combine a numbered score for every assignment into a comprehensive grade, connecting what's measured with how classes are managed.

From society we can draw a clue about the value of different approaches. People measure the level they want to manage. Grasping either aspect informs us about the other. Looking at what we measure, we say, "It looks like that's what I'm controlling for." Or we look at our outcomes, and reason back: "This should be what I'm measuring for." A relationship between these activities arises in finance, government, military, technology, and social affairs. If you want to tax dollars, that's what you measure, one dollar at a time. Precise control depends on precise measurement.

In U.S. education's familiarization system, targets often have amorphous edges that scatter energy. A diagnostic test can help us assign a student to a particular course (measurement informing management), but the correlation between the two may diverge in much instruction. What we count up in students' results may not be translated into what we ask them to do next. Noting a poor score on a quiz, the teacher says, "You need to work harder on that section." Harder? Okay, sure. Yes, ma'am. The purpose of the test has been accomplished—the teacher has made a comparative judgment of the student—but the class is moving on to the next section, and the fact that the student got five wrong is not a follow-up concern (measurement not informing management).

Measure conditions instead of events. For an objective, valid, and reliable basis of scoring, I've proposed the criterion that students explain their knowledge to another without help and retain it, applicable K–12. If you have twenty points you want them to master, your scoring system is straightforward. *Count up those they can explain and those they can't and ask them to master the latter*, so that measurement and management align. Credit them only for what's risen to and remains at the criterion.

The distinction between measuring an event versus a condition is crucial for resolving the confusion around testing. An event is surface, a condition deep. The first reports on a slice of time, the second on the collection of many such slices. The first is about temporary effort, the second about ongoing effort. The first describes a moment's assertion; the second, a pattern of assertions. Note the difference between these two teacher expectations:

> "Remember the answer on test day." By this measure, it doesn't worry us that they don't know it right *before* test day nor just *after* test day but only *on* test day, nor that even to achieve this much we offer them hints

and review questions, encourage their cramming, and guide their effort to improve their answers. We can afford to make our measurement superficial because we've already committed to conditions that provide only the appearance of validity. Our measurement and management match perfectly.

Instead, consider the alternative.

"Remember the answer for six months after you last looked at it." Imagine saying to them:

> Class, you'll be surprised to learn that the depth of your grasp of any learning can be measured in accurate numbers. Just count up how many days after you last looked at it that you can still remember it completely. So if you had a test on Monday and the material is disappearing by Wednesday, that's two-day retention. By Wednesday you're already losing it. With thirty-day retention, you could pass the same test in another month as well as you can today.
>
> We're going to try to help you obtain six-month retention, building a permanent mastery of a field of knowledge, learning it so thoroughly that you can explain it when I ask you again in six months.

That outcome depends on a relatively easy instructional change any teacher can make. Follow me here.

READMINISTER COMPREHENSIVE TESTS

Tests currently reflect knowledge at a particular time instead of what's maintained, making it easier to subvert them with study methods that rely on rapid input followed by forgetting. By measuring knowledge that will be intentionally dismissed after the test, we create a false picture of what a student continues to know.

A score becomes more valid when applied to what students maintain cumulatively. To find that out we do two things. *We give comprehensive tests and readminister them till students know them perfectly.* Before discussing these steps, however, let me suggest a context.

Above we noted six qualities that make a score more versus less useful *to the student*. A single decision helps us toward that value—that we return to teachers designing the test themselves based on what they have taught. A test should essentially extend communication between teacher and students, be *for* students' use, directly reflect their immediately preceding effort, arrive immediately, be objective and accurate, and be socially valued. Developing the test, the teacher knows exactly where class effort has progressed, and *only because of this* knows what's appropriate to ask on the test.

If others want to know something about students, *they should find out in a way that doesn't interfere with the results they want*—interference not the least of which is the enormous time and effort given to tests that are of little use to students.

Ignoring this principle has opened a minefield of arguments—how important is standardized testing compared with all other uses of teacher and student time; whether all should know the same basics; if so, who should define them; and how closely teachers should "teach to" them. And is it *possible* to define a body of knowledge that's right for the entire nation? In trying to do that, what do we sacrifice? What place should be given to teacher initiative, variance in student readiness, and the multiple ways new information reaches awareness?

Should we, can we even, machine-grade students to reveal who's teaching well or poorly, and what should we do with that information? Should we fear standardization or embrace it enthusiastically? And will teachers want to teach in the system that results?

In the sectors of our lives that we navigate with common sense, I suggest that when faced with deciding among uncertainties, we gravitate in the end to what we're surest of. One thing we're sure of is that assessment can be helpful when used as a tool between teacher and students to guide actual effort. The further we depart from that context, the more vulnerable we are to big mistakes.

For now we're stuck with accommodating to a mainstream belief that comprehensive tests tell you something. If we could at least allow tests to be created by teachers on the basis of what students have worked to learn, how might we leverage them for better results? Two steps could make a difference:

Give comprehensive tests that include everything of value covered since the last test. These would be the most challenging students could face about the material, and hence warrant all the practice and help leading up to them. A high score would mean that the student actually knew the material on test day.

Doing this much, however, isn't enough. It achieves an imprint on a student's mind but not like the single glance of a gosling on a mother goose that lasts a lifetime. It's more like a child's writing in beach sand before an incoming tide. Unless moved to safer ground, *goodbye imprint!* A high school health teacher shook his head as he showed me a test he'd mistakenly given a second time. None of his students noticed they'd had the identical test two weeks before. For a permanent imprint, all we need is this:

Readminister all previous tests on randomly selected, unannounced days. As individual students demonstrate sustained mastery, exempt them from further testing on a particular section. For all others, continue retesting all old material and make their last score of the series their course grade.

An easy, time-efficient way to do this is to find a small pocket of regular time—say, twenty minutes max—a couple of days a week when you can readminister a single, brief, randomly selected section from a prior test.

This would spur students to study efficiently and to pace themselves for long-term learning. It would be easy for the teacher since using the same test would require no further preparation. Students hear, "Bring this up to mastery as soon as you can and keep it there." They'd steadily tuck away mastery without the pressure of big tests and would just improve continually.

One might object, "But they'll just learn the answer without thinking through all the material."

The objection holds if the test is superficial or only samples what's taught. If instead we make it comprehensive and they master it, *that's what we want*. We want it so complete that if students get only what's in it, they master the course. I find personally that when I learn any specific chunk thoroughly, I'm more likely actually to think about it later and associate it with other ideas.

Learning the answer thoroughly isn't a downside but rather a step firmly achieved. If you're going to teach to the test, which *designedly happens everywhere* either explicitly or subtly, at least have it contain the learning you want and then really learn it. In a mature system, we trust teachers to teach effectively, know what they have taught and students have learned, understand what's important to test, and then design the test.

The randomness in retesting is key. Scheduling a test beforehand affects the learning from it. If students see it coming, their scores from it are less valid. Foreknowledge of the test day makes cramming inevitable, enabling students repeatedly to pass a test with superficial understanding. If the selection of the day and the section instead is unforeseen and students never know when they'll be asked which questions, they'll know they must master everything, must be constantly ready to explain assigned knowledge.

Remember what it takes to get permanent knowledge—first mastery and then distributed recall. To carry a piece forward, first identify it, cast it in a condensed but complete summary with examples as needed, and treat it like a nest egg you guard because you want it to hatch. Most learning about most subjects decays rapidly because not recalled periodically.

SUMMARY

1. Scoring energizes effort of all kinds.

2. We can design scoring to motivate students or undermine their motivation.
3. Make your measurement useful for what you manage.
4. Measure deep conditions instead of passing events.
5. Teach so students remember it six months later.
6. Readminister comprehensive tests randomly, section by section, so students maintain their mastery of all prior work.
7. Teachers should design tests based on what they teach.
8. If students don't know when they'll be tested, they're spurred to maintain all their learning.
9. Scheduling tests ensures that much of the score is based on cramming and is soon lost.
10. Create condensed, complete summaries of subjects, and recall them periodically.

TWELVE

More Ways to Use Scoring: Tracking Progress on Many Fronts

Score retained knowledge. To estimate the knowledge students actually retain ongoing, we need to measure differently than if we're satisfied with what they know at a given moment. The difference is our insistence on maintained knowledge.

Organize material into questions and answers as is already done. Then students practice explaining them until they can do so without prior review. Wait to apply a final score on a piece until they can tell it back at any time.

This simplifies assessment. A single criterion that applies continually relieves us of relying on high-pressure events. Since the standard is valid every day, we can check in on section five today, two tomorrow, and nine on Wednesday. It doesn't matter when because students realize that we expect them to know all of them steadily. Ongoing retention offers a clear line in the sand. Their ability to explain something back is a yes/no standard and hence the basis for an objective, quantitative measure — valid, cumulative, and replicable classroom to classroom.

For scores to be reliable, we need a basic unit size, a building block aligned with students' capacity. Teachers home in on an appropriate size as they present and test knowledge, and alight on the chunk that fits their pupils so that questions on a test are of comparable difficulty.

How many new notes of information should we aim for in the basic unit? Few minds can simultaneously attend to more than seven at once, though our comfort zone is smaller.[31] We do well with one or two. We perceive the one, the two we connect up — a new subject and verb, say — or go up to three with a subject, verb, and modifier absorbed together.

The unit instinctively preferred appears to be a clause or sentence containing two to five novel notes of meaning, each a single word or number, as our cellular unit (see note 9 about the limited few "slots" in working memory). In sentences of several words, the new pieces are the words that stretch knowledge. Known words supply the context and new ones extend it. To identify a unit of score, think in terms of what you'd ask in a comprehensive test and the level of detail you'd expect to mark off if your students miss it.

COUNT QUANTITY

Once you have settled upon a scoring unit appropriate for subject and students, you can count up its reliable, replicable quantity. Add up each detail mastered—four of them here, twelve there, twenty-three in that section. If a question has five parts or steps, we give them a score of five *to keep* and don't score it again because we expect them to retain the first one. Each unit of score amounts to a claim that they know one point continuously and hold onto the score only if they hold onto the knowledge.

Apply this especially to categories of details like the significant terms of a subject. Two hundred and fifty of them in a middle school math glossary are a fitting year-long project. Post a chart on the wall to track each student's progress, and carve off the terms one at a time with instruction and practice. When students learn one, have them explain it to another who verifies that they know it, tally their accomplishment by their name, and periodically practice the terms back to the beginning.

Science is stuffed with categories: technical terms, steps of processes, formulas, Latin names of living things and their characteristics, parallel parts of a whole, stages of a sequence, or factors in a problem. Or English grammar: At your students' level, identify the set pieces you want them to have perfectly like uses of a comma, capitalizations, types of sentences, and grammar rules. A rule plus three examples warrants a score of four.

Any specific and exact learning has the same requirement for mastery—first understand it and then practice it. Learn, save. Then account for progress with scoring. Just mastering the basics, every high school graduate should be able to write at least correctly if not elegantly. The price of doing this is just being specific about the pieces comprising a chunk and counting them as they're mastered.

Compare this to constructing a test and giving separate value to increments representing independent effort. In complex questions with multiple parts, steps, or features, each merits a unit of score. As each is learned, applied correctly, and accounted for, students know they are on track— where their knowledge stops and where to focus next. If a part requires effort to learn and isn't embedded in or implied by another, it deserves a score, as does one that would be marked off if missed on a test but is correct.

Getting a score for a piece done right lets the student reward himself with a sense of progress and the realization that his effort paid off, encouraging him to do the same with another piece. He notes that the effort in the prior step is about the same in the next. It's portioned out in bite-sized chunks that won't overwhelm him.

Grades tell students how they're *judged* while the approach above coincides with both their effort and sense of competence with the knowledge. Because students currently aren't assessed for continuous conscious mastery, it's harder for them to know what they know. Their score is their claim that they know this piece—a different sensation than getting credit for it.

BEYOND FOLLOWING INSTRUCTIONS

Understand this partly in contrast. Many schools appear more interested in compliance than mastery. Judging by the behavior most often required, *following instructions* is the supreme skill. Graduates have adapted for years to others' directions so that a diploma guarantees rule following. Students learn to accept that others with power over them tell them what to do, and transfer this expectation to adult society, where others take advantage of their ignorance.

A score *only for consciously retained knowledge* means that if they're asked the question, they can demonstrate the answer. They notice how they lose a point as they permit it to drift off, and practice that one again. Scoring every part of an answer that took independent effort to learn, we make the charted score a direct report of their successful effort, expressing validly the difference in their output of energy on questions having many parts compared to those with one.

Posting scores beside their name encourages them to proceed and draws on the group norm that it's a good thing to show up well before one's peers. This especially helps students initially discouraged at learning. It can kick-start their motivation to discover that their effort obtains certifiable results even if they resisted doing it.

Although not all learning may reach this standard, students' maintained mastery paints an accurate picture of the whole. From their learning at that level, a teacher can easily write up an individualized academic mastery report for each student.[32] List subjects and sections treated, and for each the number of points of knowledge in it that the student can demonstrate at any time.

SKILL RATING

Allied with scoring is skill rating: checking progress toward a goal. Noting a behavior they want to improve at, students monitor their use of it.

My then-wife and I used this with communications when we were invited to conduct a two-week workshop in a distant city for a church group threatened with breakup. When we arrived a few weeks after our first contact, its board met and welcomed us to sit in.

The meeting was so constructive that I was taken aback. Later I drew one of the members aside and asked her, "How could you possibly be having problems when you have that quality of discussion on the board?"

She smiled, drew a paper from her pocket, and handed it to me. It was a list of ten skills titled Successful Group Communication I'd sent to them weeks before.

"We just put this in front of us and follow it during our meeting," she said. Monitoring themselves against a checklist of skills had a cumulative impact.

Humans enjoy setting goals and plotting progress toward them. The pleasure arises, I believe, from the innate valuing process. From infancy we try to figure out how to meet our needs. At first we rely on adults to direct us but quickly sense our own energy. We pose an idea, begin our effort, and then check ourselves. "How am I doing?," we wonder, and look for confirmation that we're on track.

Some of the power of this tendency lies not in the importance of the goal but just in the appearance of progress. Children often attach significance to what to an adult seems barely worth a glance, like their games with play materials. Finding any edge where they can improve, they typically run it as far as they can—note the sports field and computer games. Especially when success is objectively calculable as an increment of effort, their interest may become intense, and they wail when told to stop.

Even in activities of indifferent value, the question "Am I getting there?" hangs over us. If our indicators say no progress or we're falling back, we may give up and our feelings turn frustrated. So after being told for years, "You're not doing well," it shouldn't surprise us that students decide to bag formal learning. What is a C grade, after all?

Because measuring and plotting progress by itself appears rewarding, we can use it to motivate students even when they don't see the intrinsic value of what they do. We can calculate their progress on nearly any ongoing activity and point it out to them, and they accord it significance by comparing theirs with others'.

If we can, we want to focus on what already occurs rather than proposing something to try. With activities they've already begun, we sidestep the issue of *whether* to do it. They're doing it now so we're past that. Set ahead of them instead as something to try, they may think, "but I might fail," or "that means more effort," or "trying means giving in to this person who wants me to do it." When already making progress, the objections don't hold. Point out to them when they did what you ask, and now you're just scoring it.

What we measure conveys our values. By focusing on details, we declare that even differences this small matter. If we ignore them, how can we credibly claim they're important? What gets attention is what's valued. Witness technology. We focus on a nanoparticle when a nanoparticle matters.

We assert the value of microdetails by measuring them accurately and drawing on them. If they don't matter, we don't go there, and the same holds with social affairs. The level of cause and effect we study implies that (1) this *kind* of detail is important and (2) we draw on it by noting its exact application.

In my pilot project with a fractious fourth grade,[33] many instances of the motivating force of such measures stood out.

The teacher and I had been showing students how to check and rate themselves on their use of specific communication skills. One day he excitedly related an incident. As the boys played a team game, from the sidelines he heard loud voices, usually the prelude to a fist fight. He hurried to the group in time to hear one of the worst fighters say to another, "So you're saying that . . ." and summarize his words. In a minute they had talked out the problem and resumed the game. The teacher was beaming. We were making a difference.

I developed the list they used from extensive observation in K–12, inviting students to try out different versions in small-group discussions. Not all items fit every age level, but conveying the list to the limit of students' understanding takes them as far as they can go.

It's easy to underrate their interest. Attending one of my trainings in a remote Alaska town was a teacher who decades before had been National Teacher of the Year, living there for her husband's scientific work. After I'd introduced the skills list to the staff, I visited her classroom. Her fifth graders had been upset, she told me, upon discovering that they didn't know the skills already. She assigned them to learn the entire list by heart, which they did eagerly.

ACTIVITIES TO SCORE

As we've noted, many students are credited just for the motions of an activity rather than for its results. The less a behavior correlates with actual learning, the less its value. To remove obscurity, identify the details that register precisely what you want—the metric, the calculable development of skill or knowledge. If you see a behavior among students that you want to change, begin by counting it to establish a baseline.

Even if you don't know yet how to make the change, if you measure accurately what registers progress in it, you've begun. Attention to the measure lets everyone know its importance, spurring them to find an intervention that alters it.

The best measures are a single figure that sums up a mix of skills so that each integer of score reveals exercise of the set. "The race to the moon" drew on an entire nation's human and technological skill, and a single run in baseball can occur by an arcane combination of abilities. Watch for cues telling you whether the measure meets students' needs and stimulates learning.

The activities below lend themselves to objective measurement. Sometimes you assign a score, but often students monitor their own or each other's progress.

1. Kindergarten and primary grade students needing basic skills are especially anxious to have their effort count. They want to see effort–success–effort–success. They can play a game for hours without taxing their supposedly limited attention span.

What they don't like is wasted time. They want to know the right action, do it, and be told they're on track. Adults need to point them toward what advances their capacity for more complex tasks. How, for example, can we plot beginning reading skills? Imagine a chart with a couple dozen columns and a row for every student. Each column corresponds to a category of details you want them to master, such as:

Column 1. Alphabet. Every student can work up to a perfect score of twenty-six.
Column 2. Vowels separately (a-e-i-o-u-y)
Column 3. A couple dozen alternate sounds for the vowels.
Column 4. Six words ending in *-ight*
Column 5. Ten words containing *-ish*
Column 6. Eight words beginning in *wh-*
Column 7. Ten words beginning in *th-*
Column 8. Five words ending in *-ay*
Column 9. Ten words ending in *-tion*

Any column can be devoted to a set of specific learning such as prefixes, suffixes, rules of grammar and punctuation, and an array of math definitions and problem-solving sequences. Where students' ability varies, form balanced teams with top students as their captains, each helping one or more of the less skilled, and chart every team's total score.

2. A simple measure for early elementary students is minutes reading, a score they can increase whenever they have time. Beginning a period, say, "Please start reading," and time them collectively. Seeing anyone distracted, adjust their score accordingly, letting everyone know that *eve-*

ry second of their reading matters—to you if not to them. Even if the measure isn't perfect, it reflects their focus. Knowing that you might monitor them personally spurs attention and record keeping. As they grasp the method, they can time themselves or sit with a partner who does it.

If most of your students read anyway when you ask them to, why bother with a measure?

While some read to please you and others actually enjoy it, a third group views it as free time. They comply as they must, but their drives for relationship, self-expression, and distractive thoughts interfere. Many also face problems of understanding that delay them. Measuring *their competence at concentrating on reading* may be just enough added motive to keep them focused. When they all do this well, you can suspend any rating method used to get them going.

3. Working with immigrants who had severe deficits in reading English, I found words read a helpful measure. Early in their learning, every word sounded out, pronounced correctly, and understood was a victory. These they gladly counted up as their achievement for the day and were pleased to have it posted. This applied not only to reading new material but also to rereading previously grasped though still poorly mastered words.

4. Score their writing in notes, reports, and journals by words written. It's objective, takes only a few seconds for them to count, and can be posted cumulatively. For typewritten assignments later, computer programs count words for them. In their journal, they may want to count words themselves, but asking partners to do this for each other may aid accuracy, increase significance, and provide a motive to produce something.

Each day they add new numbers to their total. Even if most students don't appear to need this to increase their output, it may be a decisive nudge for some. The category itself is important because the sheer quantity of their writing probably drives improvement the most. Practice makes permanent.

5. A basic measure is time on task, time doing class work. With distracted students, it's also a way to describe their behavior to a parent or administrator, especially if volunteers or aides are assigned according to needs, and it's valuable information for students themselves. List names on a dry-erase board. At every break or whenever changing their activity, run quickly down the list and give each your best estimate of their degree of cooperation plotted as minutes or a percentage. If they argue about their score, this *helps* because it means that the score matters to them enough that they want to raise it. Negotiate a fair estimate with them and continue.

To do this with a high school class exhibiting a spectrum of cooperation, I created a check sheet on four measures: distracting others, ignoring requests, being on task, and being off task. I randomly tallied what they appeared to be doing and in a half day gave ninety checks, averaging one every two minutes for three hours.

Several students seemed motivated by their scores, yet the usual suspects relapsed into familiar distractions. Thinking they might respond better to the overall percentage of time they focused on productive tasks, I collapsed their constructive behavior into a single measure, producing a ranking from a high of 90 percent to a low of 20 percent.

When I was ready to present my findings, they gave me rapt attention. I pointed out how important it was to apply good ideas to their lives and that the scores I assigned them weren't a judgment but rather objective feedback. I asked one student if the 80 percent I assigned him was accurate—the proportion of his time focused on work and otherwise relaxing or chatting. He thought it was fair.

The others then wanted me to read off everyone's score. A couple felt they deserved adjustments I accepted as fair, although the constructive time spent by the bottom half of the list was mainly at gardening, exercise group, and music practice, with little on academics. Typically they were sitting, wandering around the premises, going to the bathroom, getting a drink, joking, watching someone else, or talking. Feedback on where they stood individually on the scale startled them and appeared to stimulate study. Continued daily, the measure would likely show a gradual rise in the daily average even apart from staff's determination to nail laggards.

6. For peer reinforcement in the primary grades, make a chart with all their names listed and three large columns titled "Helpful," "Focused," and "Friendly." Periodically invite students to go to the chart and place a tally mark under any category as feedback to another student.

Giving it a lighthearted spin, consider using it even for senior high students when you encounter them parched for appreciation. Some may show up more helpful and others more focused, and you'll get them weighing what helpfulness adds to being friendly.

7. To encourage their collective cooperation, you might offer students a presumptive five minutes bonus time hourly to use according to their group choice. They might save it up for an hour of games, a field trip, or a movie or take time off early at recess or lunch.

To earn it they need only respond when you say, "Class!" or "Could I have everyone's attention?" Count to five, and if everyone is quiet, faces you, and begins the activity you request, they save their bonus time, but they lose it for the amount of time they continue distracting. Do the same when they interrupt an ongoing activity. Measure their distraction time throughout the day and subtract the total from their bonus time.

This practice helps the group influence the least focused, giving it a reason to nudge them to comply so everyone can receive the payout. Conditions that aid this approach are that they accept each other, consequences aren't extreme, they feel only a slight pinch from others' distractive behavior, and no one is alienated from the group.

As much as you can, influence behavior by minimal consequences—small results barely uncomfortable and barely noticed but fair and consistent. Big ones are more likely to elicit resentment or rebellion and make you less likely to apply them consistently.

8. If students protest that they can't corral the remaining distracters and if it's not too complicated, apply consequence time to the problem behavior of the few. It can help to be accurate and to manifest a lighthearted spirit like you would bring to a game. Reward positive behavior reliably and apply consequences to negative behavior. Accurately and fairly, some lose privileges awarded to others. Erratic reward and punishment diminish their incentive to cooperate. Make extremely clear (1) your signal for order, (2) a record of their individual compliance, and (3) proportionate consequences.

You might list all names on a 3-x-5 card you keep in your pocket, and explain:

> When I say "class" and raise my hand, I'll count to five. Then I'll take out my list and make a tally beside the name of anyone who continues to distract. Once a week, or when I collect some tallies, we'll have rewards and consequences.

Brainstorm with them a set of each. They will be happy to tell you how they would like to be rewarded and the consequences others should receive for not cooperating.

9. Measure delay time. When her high school students delayed in returning from lunch and recess, a teacher quickly increased their cooperation. She timed their delay to the second and added it to when they would be dismissed for the day.

10. Rough in communication skills. All you need are (1) clear identification of the desired behavior and (2) recognition of when it occurs. You might select six to eight behaviors and print them above columns on a chart with student names down the side. The following are all observable: Look at speaker, leave a brief silence (don't interrupt), connect to others' ideas, ask questions, speak clearly and firmly, summarize others' ideas, give a compliment.

You need not say a word. Just tallying behavior tells students their actions are noticed. If someone inquires, "Why are you doing that?," you answer, "Just keeping track." *Just keeping track*—a hint that this is important enough to warrant steady attention. Students fix on their own name and instinctively grasp how their peers see them. Think of any behavior you want more of and invent an objective signal that you've observed its use.

11. A common problem among students is maintaining a concentrated focus on schoolwork. Many want to change this but don't know how.

Our basic premise applies here, that rating anything we want to change stimulates effort toward it. Many diagnosed with ADD or ADHD who have resigned themselves to wandering attention find that a conscious, moment-by-moment self-check helps keep their mind on track.

Lay out a scale and adapt it to students' level. If you don't have graph paper, make your own by turning paper to landscape position. Draw twenty one-eighth-inch rows centered in the paper and then column lines that fill it with one-eighth-inch squares. Label the middle horizontal line 0, and number lines downward to −10 and upward to +10.

Explain to students that they can plot their concentration on the scale from low to neutral to high. With a marker, show them how to make a bold line up from the zero baseline to what they think is their high for the day and down from it to their low. You might also use a line graph to connect all their daily high scores and another for low scores. The range between their high and low gives them a visual picture of how their attention varies.

Kindergarten and lower elementary students can use a single sheet of paper with a line dividing upper and lower to show their use or misuse of a single behavior. With a bold marker, they give themselves a star in the top half or an X in the lower, or with a brief list of three or four behaviors make a tally by each one they use. The level of detail should reflect the choices they're aware of making.

For more frequent self-assessment, like checking themselves every fifteen to thirty minutes, make up a chart with a dozen narrow columns a half inch wide, number them 1 to 12, and use one column per day. Draw row lines that turn each column into a stack of half-inch square boxes in which students can jot their self-ratings through the course of the day.

To start, point them to the top square in column 1 and enter there how they rate their focus from 1 to 100 percent for the past hour. Until they can do it on their own, help them make an accurate self-rating every half hour down the same column.

12. Score learning directly with minutes explaining. They pair up and time each other in minutes and seconds as they summarize a question treated. A partner varied daily confirms and posts their time for a particular unit on a dry-erase board or acetate-covered chart. As with counting written words, this measure provides them a peer-based reason to think intentionally all day.

Minutes explaining is a useful metric for their learning of history, literature, and social studies. Anything that has a beginning, middle, and end or forms into a narrative is better explained as such than chopped up into points. And in any subject, when students have already accumulated basic factual information, further improvement in their thinking is more likely from explaining, along with discussion or other challenges you pose for them.

For inclusion in their academic mastery report, the minutes they take to explain every section of their learning constitute a valid record of ability.

13. Score learning with points of knowledge. Have students count up all the details they learn, one at a time, by the criterion of what they can tell a questioner without help. All knowledge qualifies that would be marked off as a mistake if gotten wrong on a test, but instead of waiting for mistakes, we count what they can explain correctly. Each new piece deserves a point of new score, a correlation perfectly reflecting the effort they expend.

Once they understand how to apply the measures themselves, they can take charge of them and know that their measures hold true. Teachers tally and post results, and everyone knows the entire class accomplishment, which also can be used for class-to-class competition. Outcomes are unarguable because demonstrable.

If you have an hour's presentation, stop after ten minutes and ask students to identify the key elements so far (e.g., two new terms and three points explained). Write them down and organize them neatly so everyone acquires a perfect model to that point. As you complete new chunks, students practice them at once.

In subjects where you can't immediately assign problems to solve, pair up students. Tell them to ask each other the question(s) you've treated and raise their hand when their partner answers perfectly. Scoring their progress helps focus them where their effort matters most.

14. Count up naturally occurring key sequences. Math and science usually offer something to do with a new idea: Solve a problem, make an application, do an experiment, set up a project, connect it to something else. There's an action set. Softer subjects may offer no obvious action so it's up to you to propose one, such as dividing the material into chunks and starting students on their way to permanent mastery.

Any handful of selected skills can be your focus. The seven listed under Perfect Conversation in chapter 9 have broad application. Select *observable* behaviors that manifest the development you want, and arrange for students to check themselves or each other on them daily.

One student I worked with had trouble with long division. His teacher, a determined lady with a large class, explained math principles as a flow: this means this, and remember this, and then it becomes this, and then you change this to that, and, and . . . At some point this student had apparently given up after missing some steps. He was confused about microquestions like,

1. What words in a problem tell you to divide to find the answer?
2. What's the name of each of the numbers in a division problem?
3. For a division problem on a page, how do you describe what you see?

4. Encountering a division sign in a problem, how do you place correctly the numbers before and after it inside or outside the bracket for dividing?
5. What do you do first when the number in front of the bracket has a decimal?
6. When do you use estimating?
7. How do you know what number to put first on top of the bracket?
8. Where *exactly* do you place it?
9. When do you use multiplying in a division problem?
10. When do you use subtracting?
11. When do you bring down the next number?
12. Where do you bring it down to?
13. What do you do after you bring down a number?

With these mastered from the start, he'd have accumulated thirteen points of knowledge about division, so why not teach them? I assume schools believe it's not a good use of time, that most don't need microsteps. But if this student is blocked, why not provide a backup for him? When I reached him, he gave up easily and felt he just couldn't understand. Learning the microsteps helped him turn a corner.

To ensure everyone's success at long division, have a chart just for the thirteen points. List students' names with thirteen columns beside them. Explain the points, assign partners to practice them, tally their mastery of each point as they learn it, and apply the steps to problems.

15. Use such a chart to break down new concepts you present. Separate as a point of knowledge *every step of a sequence where they might make a mistake*, anywhere it takes effort to get it right. When they reach the end of a math process, they'll do the whole thing with confidence that they know each phase and score their gains. Do this with each new chunk, and save all previous ones.

If this seems extra work for you, remember how they're almost obsessed as they score other activities. The critical role of a score is connecting effort directly to success—customarily perceived as giving a right answer. At first answers are one word and later maybe a thirty-minute discourse on a principle of physics. Level determines complexity. Detail-exact mastery within a context moves them beyond vague, recognition-based learning, and scoring it informs them unmistakably, "You're doing it!"

16. Give more form to learning saved. "Class, let's keep a list of all the questions you can answer." Their interest in posting results at a day's end moves them to keep track. Make scores most useful by counting up the subpoints under every question. In the way one would score a comprehensive test, do the same for each separate step that takes learning effort.

In questions containing a sequence, parts of a whole, or points of development, any one part missing would receive a single mark off, but instead of waiting for the mistake, we credit them up front for learning it.

Instead of registering their total effort this way, however, teachers customarily mark off just the final answer of a multistep problem, a shortcut serving their own need rather than the student's. Scoring is more useful to the latter as it credits every independent step. Students feel intuitively that a sixteen-step process deserves a sixteen-point score—one for every step where effort at learning forestalled a wrong answer.

17. To master math concepts, an online contributor writes, "The old star system still works." He paces progress these ways: List on a wall chart or computer program the most important concepts students will face in state and NCLB testing, and post a star by their names as they master them. Use pre- and posttesting for selecting subject matter and assessing progress.

Announce to the class when someone masters a concept. Use peer tutors. Have many ways to recognize progress such as award certificates or pencils printed with "Good work" or "Star Student." Order them in bulk and use them year to year. Send home "Your Child Is a Star" success cards for each concept mastered, telling what it was. Explain the concepts in a letter to parents at the beginning of school. Encourage progress short of mastery with positive feedback to parents. Have an occasional "Star party." Review old concepts to make sure students retain everything.

SUMMARY

1. Organize material into questions and answers, and have students practice it in pairs till they know it.
2. Score it once, expect them to retain it, and requestion it at random intervals.
3. Knowledge enters a few available slots in working memory, which discards them in less than a minute unless a further step is taken.
4. We can count up all the points of knowledge students know—each detail that would be counted off if missed on a test.
5. Make a scoring chart for any specific body of knowledge you want all students to maintain, such as math terms.
6. Score only for consciously retained knowledge.
7. Scoring also with self- and other-ratings on skills spurs motivation.
8. If possible, use scoring on what they already do rather than what they haven't yet begun.
9. Use it for basic reading skills, minutes reading, words read, words written, time on task, friendship skills, cooperation time, consequence time, bonus time, communication skills, concentrated focus, minutes explaining, points of knowledge, key sequences,

breaking down new concepts, all the questions they can answer, and "the old star system."

THIRTEEN

Practice by Performance: The Motivational Spur from Performing

Children are nodes of attention-getting. Because they seek it so avidly, their views of each other are probably our most powerful ally if we can harness them. They love to show off what they can do, which prompts them to do more. We want to arrange their activity so it both serves learning and impresses their peers.

ENGAGING PEER INFLUENCE

Few schools *enlist* peer influence. Often students instead are literally afraid of appearing smart because their peers discount it. Adults blame students for this, but it's a reasonable outcome of school policies that define some effort as success and other effort as not good enough.

Think about it. Students invest only in standards they believe they can aspire to. If they're labeled a C student or consigned to a competitive rather than cooperative system, they may find themselves in a stable cohort that resents others with a more attractive label. This moves them to seek out other means of significance that may not please us.

I had an eye-opening conversation with a five-year-old about this. He had just deliberately ruined the work of another five-year-old and stood over her as though gloating, and staff were puzzled. But this was a bright kid. Believing he was *reasoning*, I tried to follow it carefully and mirrored his thinking while watching him for clues.

"Okay," I said to him, "'when I ruin others' work . . . everyone is mad at me and when everyone is mad at me . . . *I'm really important!*'"

At that point he broke into a smile and nodded vigorously. We set about finding other ways he could be important.

Performance is a present-time dynamic that celebrates today anyone who stands up and demonstrates learning. Our collective attention to immediate self-expression bypasses differences in overall quantity of knowledge. The class applauds a student's effort right now to stand and show off one chunk.

We can distinguish the admiration we want from simple attention. The latter is positive in its own way though I suspect schools don't weigh carefully the gain from the time spent. Assemblies may recognize students for what costs them no effort, such as having a birthday. There's merit in letting them know we regard them benevolently and they should be able to count on affirmation just for being alive. Any of us are encouraged when people tell us, "Good job!," regardless of our actual productivity.

ANSWERING QUESTIONS

Admiration is a stronger potion. It's based on respect for effort that achieves something, and its impact is important enough to plan how to engage it. First we generate a competence that *deserves* attention. Second, we prepare a setting to respond favorably to it, typically by applause. Knowing it will be their turn any moment, students willingly clap for each other.

We can arrange both these conditions around answering questions. By their practice at it, students ensure that they'll do it successfully. We then tap the latent motivational juice through a slightly formal demonstration of it, enough to give the student a sensation of rising to the occasion.

Doing this periodically, students also employ the spaced intervals that deepen retention while adding a lively tone. This can be significant because as children we start off life believing that everything should be exciting even as repeated experiences settle us into a routine. Then as adults we exert effort that doesn't *feel* successful even if it's necessary. Performance restores the pizzazz.

Sports where a coach guides a team offer a parallel. If their coach understands the effort that makes a difference, students get better at it privately and display it in public. By practice, team members buy into the coach's strategy and support each other.

In the classroom team, students do so willingly but not by accident. Except for the occasional group project that students often object to when others' contributions don't match their own, few schools teach students *how to affirm each other's effort.*

Instead of operating by team dynamics, teachers themselves manage every step of learning, with student self-expression more often a threat to good order than a resource to tap. Even if students master a segment of knowledge, there's seldom an opportunity to display it publicly because, as ordinarily conceived, this would require too much classroom time.

Our aim, however, isn't to fill up time performing but rather to draw on its motivational properties to spur preparation. The *expectation* of performance, and the social relations it implies, give meaning to the effort leading to it. Performance done even for a few minutes at day's end can season an entire day.

Note contrasting views about this. One teacher does her standard activities day by day, realizes students are lackadaisical and bored, and in casting around for a way to spice things up, suddenly declares, "All right, we're going to have a performance of what you know." The result is anxiety and resistance, and most importantly there is *no use of performance to spur preparation.*

Another teacher tells students, "Every Tuesday and Friday for five minutes at 3:10 p.m. I'm going to draw questions we've worked on and names of people to spring to their feet and answer them." Performance *foreseen* spurs preparation.

To appreciate the motivation involved, recall when you were first asked to give a talk in public. Invited perhaps weeks or months ahead, how did the subject rest on your mind? It energized you. You may even have obsessed about it, but although you might have discussed it with others, the main work was internal. You had to think about it. You had to make sense of it and consider how a flow of words could accomplish the purpose of your talk.

SINGLE POINT TO START

The most casual beginning could go like this. With three minutes remaining you draw five names at random. Each in turn stands, and you ask them a single question dealt with throughout the day. When they respond correctly, you lead everyone in applause.

Even a few performing what they recall sets a tone and encourages you to identify specifically the ideas you want them to keep in mind. It need not take long because you don't have to hear from everyone. Just knowing they *might* be invited to do this can spur students to think all day about it.

You can ask for longer retention and turn it into a game: "If you can remember an idea from yesterday, you get two points instead of one and three for a point from three days ago." Draw as many names as you have time for, keep score of their progress with tallies, and turn the tallies into chances in a raffle drawing for M&M's. The result will be that *they think all day about the point they'll remember.*

SELF-LIMITATIONS

Speaking to the class, however, stresses many students. I estimate that two-thirds of students carry one or more limiting attitudes such as self-consciousness, sensitiveness to criticism, fear of failure, worry, or self-underestimation. These can affect their lives so profoundly that turning them around deserves major attention. We want them able to perform despite their fear and take their seat afterward saying, "Well, I *nailed* it."

Fortunately, it's easy to make performance successful and students confident by practice beforehand. They explain the material several times to another student until they have it mastered; rough in the ideas, assign words to them, and smooth them into an intelligible flow. They steadily increase their confidence till they realize, "I can do this." When they rise to their feet to perform to the class, competence kicks in and they carry out the whole set—not only the answer they practiced but also its self-image and attitudinal features. The excitement of the performance carries them through the personal work leading up to it. It's much like a course in public speaking except that the topics are the entire academic curriculum.

STANDARD SEQUENCE

Conceiving instruction as woven into a performance dynamic, we begin with new material by teacher explanation, handouts, texts, graphics, media clips, discussions, or projects. The content is broken into questions students can answer, and they practice them with a partner until both know them and maintain all past questions.

Slightly different steps occur if your class is homogeneous and everyone learns at the same pace. Then, a single set of questions for performance works well by the following steps:

1. Identify a question you want mastered.
2. Students practice it to the point of confidence in their answer.
3. You write the question on a slip with the answer available in hard copy in their notes or materials.
4. Drop the slips in a bag.
5. Set a regular time for a performance.
6. Draw a question randomly, read it, and pause a moment.
7. Draw the name of a student who stands and performs it.
8. The class applauds.

Some steps differ if all students aren't working on the same thing. Perhaps your students vary in age, ability, or confidence; or they work on different subjects, or at different points in the same one, or at their own pace, or you welcome material from outside reading or interests. In such cases, all have their own bag. Once they're confident of performing a point—whether from personal or class material—the question goes onto a slip and into their personal bag. At performance time, a name is drawn first, and the student hands his or her bag to the teacher or another student who draws a question from it.

The second step above, practice, is crucial—indispensable. For ensuring everyone's success, we first make sure that they practice the answers with a peer who verifies that their partner knows it. Practicing even a complex answer with different partners, they reach a plateau of saturation where it requires no effort for them to give a masterful answer.

If that question comes up, they can demonstrate it with confidence. Foreseeing this, they experience satisfaction up front, enjoying the steady certainty arising from mastery. It may increase their sense of control over their learning to ask them collectively when they feel confident enough of a particular question to assign it to the class performance bag.

To save time, instead of writing each question on a slip in step three, you can number the questions in your own and students' notes. Then write just a single number on the slip you drop in the bag. For the performance, draw a number, read the question from your notes, and then draw a student's name.

RANDOM DRAWING

Step six, random drawing of the question, helps to shift energy from teacher control to a chance element. It mutes the gamelike feeling for the teacher instead to select both the question and the student to answer. Placing step six before seven, drawing a name, elicits more effort overall. You want everyone to think what they'll say if they're named, so you allow time for them to do so.

A chance drawing of the name in the seventh step helps allay an unconscious pattern teachers can fall into over who to call on and why. Because they don't *want* to give anyone a failure experience, they may steer away from calling on the very one who needs the attempt most.

It can also demand teachers' self-discipline to allow some students the added time they need to put words to their thoughts, a need better met earlier during partner practice. In their understandable desire to make a point efficiently, teachers may rely on the "knows-all-tells-all" student who has his hand up even before he hears the question.

Teachers also respond unconsciously to cues like eye contact. With head lowered, one student begs not to be called on, and with eyes front another hints, "I'm ready." Teachers may see their options as either nudging the first toward a possible failure or the second to a likely success, either way skewing the distribution of individual involvement. Reducing some students' expectation of expressing themselves then minimizes their motivation to prepare and participate.[34]

If you're thinking, "That doesn't happen to me," you might check yourself. The conditioning is largely unconscious. The students of a college psychology class, unknown to their teacher, agreed before a lecture to try to shape it just by using eye contact. By the end of the period they had steered him into an extended presentation on sexuality.

Step eight, applause for showing off mastery, is the ultimate objective. Five minutes of performance at the end of the day can cap students' feeling of success. They work hour by hour, show off a little, and go home with applause ringing in their ears.

I could be biased about this, but I believe that daily performances of learning in which every student eventually participates and succeeds produces a more valid account of conscious mastery than anything schools do with paper tests now. It corrects a mistake accepted almost universally in U.S. education—that superficial, silent, impersonal, familiarized, unexpressed learning for credits is enough. By steadily demonstrating and celebrating specific knowledge in a social arena, we observe directly what students know and interest them in pursuing more of it.

MAKING CHANGE EFFICIENT

While we want to use performance mainly to stimulate learning, a parallel element is involved also in starting and stopping activities. In any school you might encounter scenes, as I did, of seventy-five fourth graders performing an intensive series of dance exercises. They responded instantly to a stream of commands from their energetic coach, clearly enjoying the experience. *Students love efficient expression of their energy.* You can apply this principle to transitions between classroom activities, adapting the explanation below to their age and issue:

> How many have ever been on a team? When you're playing a game, there are times to start. Then you put out effort, and then stop, right? That's how games go. You rest up, and then one moment you start the game. Doing this depends on knowing the game and having someone start and stop it.
>
> So let's say we're going to have small-group discussions. We settle on a topic, assign groups, you sit somewhere with your group, and then when I give the word, you start. How long should it take from the time I explain the activity to the time you're ready to begin?
>
> There's a delay possible at every point. Maybe you don't like the topic, so you talk about that with people around you, or you *do* like the topic and start talking before the groups are formed. Maybe you don't like the group you're assigned, so you delay and see if you can be in another one; or you can't find a place to sit and wander around. You

don't listen carefully to the guidelines, so they have to be repeated, and all this time you're talking to others and not hearing the next step in the process.

We can easily eat up fifteen minutes just getting into groups and starting. So today I'm going to use a stopwatch to see how long it takes everyone to change to the next activity. I'll start by saying the exact steps I want you to take, answer any questions about them, clarify anything not clear, and when everyone's got it, I'll say, "Please start," and begin timing you.

You carry out the steps I explained, find your partners or whatever the activity involves, and turn and look at me. When all the groups are ready, I'll click the stopwatch again to see how long it took you to make that change. Then we'll begin the activity. I'll let you know your transition time, and we can decide together how to improve if we need to.

The performance aspect lies in (1) understanding the instructions clearly, (2) doing them with a burst of energy, and (3) having a way to tell if you're getting better. Students like to perform more efficiently nearly anything they have to do anyway. As their scores improve session to session, you can congratulate them and also connect their scores to the bonus time idea described in the prior chapter.

SUMMARY

1. Students invest only in standards they can aspire to.
2. Students have a need to be admired for genuine effort they expend.
3. We can arrange this around answering a question competently.
4. To use the motivational spur of performance, teachers need to value students' self-expression.
5. The expectation of performing spurs preparation.
6. Students can start with performing a single point of knowledge and work up to larger demonstrations.
7. Students' fears and self-limitations are allayed by safe practice with a single peer.
8. Performance steps: Identify questions, practice them to the point of confidence, write them on slips, drop slips in a bag, set a regular time for performance, draw a question randomly and read it, pause a moment, draw the name of a student who stands and performs it, and class applauds.
9. Random drawing of question and student encourages preparation and interest.
10. Have students "perform" any transition to make it more efficient and easy.

FOURTEEN

The High School Vise: Working around Limitations

Perhaps you're a high school teacher caught in the vise between students' inadequate preparation, on the one hand, and on the other, unreasonable pressure on you for their academic success. Since needs and pressures aren't about to change, the last thing you may want to hear is advice. You may be thinking, "Leave me alone. I'm pedaling as fast as I can."

Okay. But I would ask you to remember how easily conditions co-opt our thinking. Placed among must-dos, we tend to organize ourselves by them. Even if they're the wrong set, we rationalize our situation, struggle with the conditions, and affirm ourselves by our ability to cope with them.

The approach I'm peddling here may seem impractical, presume more freedom than you think you have, or contradict methods you believe work for you. But if my arguments are correct, you've been inhaled by a warped system. You need a different perspective with which to make rapid changes to your students' learning.

In the spirit of "If it ain't broke, don't fix it," I want to summarize what's broke. While my comments are about the system, note how they apply to your own class.

THE U.S. SYSTEM EXTINGUISHES LEARNING

You read that right. By design, the system wipes out learning. In chapter 2, I explained how this got started and listed ten features of the resulting "learn-and-lose" system. If you don't take my word for a single suggestion I make, would you consult your own eyes on the points below? They describe the impact of *the structure*, apart from students' attitudes and behaviors:

1. Courses begin and end by plan.
2. No expressed intent to learn a body of knowledge.
3. No complete hard copy retained.
4. Teaching of small pieces not integrated.
5. Recognition-based tests.
6. Personal interest usually irrelevant.
7. Pretest reviews designed to improve scores.
8. Scheduled tests encourage cramming.
9. "Final" exam declares an end point to effort.
10. Learning and nonlearning dismissed equally.

These features really exist. I don't invent them, and they probably describe your classroom. Let's think about their significance.

First we face the fact that when messages from adults conflict, students dismiss them. A sender's congruence is a minimum condition for a believable message. If adults speak out of both sides of their mouth, students assume the whole thing is a game and that a different priority such as gaming the system is time better spent.

But in a conflict between experience and advice, which has more power? Clearly the former. When experience says, "You're done!," and advice says, "Continue," students believe experience. So with the first point above, courses do begin and end. Adults don't need to tell students, "Stop studying X and go on to Y" because X disappears from their schedule and before them now is Y. They're done with X, and its learning fades. Reality itself extinguishes what they learned in X.

Consider the scope of what they intend to learn, point two above. It's presented as a series of assignments instead of learning a complete subject. In my entire undergraduate education, I can't recall anyone ever saying, "I want you to master permanently as much of this subject as you can."

Few teachers expected mastery from everyone, much less that it be permanent and comprehensive. The imagination of even really good ones typically extended only as far as their assignments. Few believe that they can inspire students toward a thirst for continuing knowledge, and only the exceptions direct students to master comprehensively even the assignments given.

One of these was Ken Koelsch, a teacher of the year in Juneau, Alaska, in the mid-nineties, teaching government at the high school. Kids lined up a dozen deep after his classes, waiting to talk to him. One day I asked to interview him.

"This is really unusual," were his first words to me as we sat down. *"No one ever talks to me about what I do best."* As he described his approach, a phrase in particular struck me: "I am *adamant* that they know their material." For him that meant comprehensive, mastered learning for students.

While we applaud such individuals, what does it say about the system that "No one ever talks to me about what I do best"? At your school, do the master teachers effectively raise the standards of everyone about them?

The issue of hard copy is the third point. Hard copy enables you to refresh and complete knowledge that's begun to deteriorate. Perhaps as important is the expectation it carries. Without a hard copy of the material, I *expect* to forget it. Even just possessing it in writing enables me to think, "I'm keeping this," retaining the option of referring to it later.

Yet students can't keep their textbooks and rarely combine handouts and written notes into an organized, comprehensive document distilling their learning. The resulting message is that all this work, all this effort, and all these assignments *are disposable*. The design extinguishes knowledge.

One can draw similar conclusions from each of the ten factors above. Unless students' experience leads them directly to learning a large quantity of knowledge and retaining it, the outcome remains a chimera. And I'll give you odds that these conditions describe your own instructional approach. Because you largely collaborate with the school plan, you also extinguish students' knowledge.

REMEDY THE PROBLEM

If you want to alter the learn-and-lose system despite your institution's commitment to courses and credits and in spite of the ten factors, you can improve instruction with a few steps you control:

1. Tell students you want them to learn as much as possible about your subject, even beyond what you yourself teach them. Enlist their interest in making their learning permanent rather than forgettable, even within current limitations. Discuss with them how every use of time and effort you and they agree on might contribute better to that outcome. This one initiative may change everything.
2. Adopt as your criterion for mastery "the ability to explain knowledge without help and maintain it." Once they realize that they can accumulate legitimate long-term learning, they vastly prefer it in place of just getting by with appearances.
3. Help them compile a comprehensive, orderly hard copy they can keep that contains everything you want them to retain permanently. Involve them in using it in every way you can until they draw on it as an extension of their mind.

4. Cease giving tests that provide clues and hints or using questions that supply more information than does the answer. Use questions that invite a complete explanation "from scratch," that encourage students to lace together networks of knowledge.
5. Steadily retest sections of your course back to the beginning, exempting only students who clearly have them mastered. Draw their course grade from their last test for each section.
6. Retest prior material without announcing it beforehand. Randomly draw the test day and the section to be tested to show that you expect them to master everything and maintain it, and that you require long-term instead of crammed and temporary knowledge.

You and I probably think differently about how students retain knowledge. My model is the weightlifter. I suspect yours is more like the jigsaw puzzle.

In working a jigsaw puzzle, once you see how pieces go together, you're done. You grasp the underlying pattern, put pieces in their respective places, and that's enough. To present a subject, you explain pieces and how they relate to each other. As students gaze at you with a bewildered expression, you inquire: "Gerald, do you get that?" He confesses that he missed a step, and you re-explain.

Doing this with all the new parts you present, you check by asking a few random questions. The quickest students shoot up their hands, everyone nods at their answer, and you trust that you got the material across. As they carry out your assignments, you're confident that they understand.

In a jigsaw world, you're finished and can go on to the next section to do the same. When a section or unit test is due, you review these points again so that your students have a shot at a passing score. Conscious effort at retention isn't an issue. A mix of assignments and miscellaneous questions and a periodic test are adequate to run the knowledge past their minds.

With this plan, you cooperate 100 percent with the learn-and-lose system. Students grasp ideas but never deepen them, don't intend to retain them permanently, and don't study for overall comprehension. The jigsaw is like much high school knowledge also in another way: *When you stress it in the slightest, it disintegrates!*

In weightlifting instead we assume that repeated, incremental effort builds muscle. Effort is applied first to the smallest units—a single pound for hand weights—and works up from there. Before long, one grasps larger weights to start a day's workout until a hundred pounds are barely a challenge.

SOLVE THESE TWO PROBLEMS

As I see it, the parallel to working up through increasing weights in-volves two problems and two only. The first is, "Do I understand this data chunk?" Do I grasp this new idea composed of three or four novel notes just presented to me in a sentence? Understanding it means I can form a coherent mental image around it and associate it to parallel knowledge. I have this jigsaw piece in hand.

Only after the first is resolved does the second problem arise: "Do I deepen this chunk?" Doing this results from one activity only—drawing on and expressing it in some form, some way, output after input.

So let's say that for ten minutes you present new ideas. First you sort them ("This one is new, and that and that, but they already have this one"), and then enter them at once into a system of effort that sinks them more deeply into the student's mind.

When students once "have it," that's the perfect time to "deepen it." Practice with an idea begins most efficiently immediately after it's pre-sented. What arrives in the mind is seized, formed within, and expressed outwardly—claiming it and placing it on a practice track that leads to permanent mastery.

What I observe in high school classrooms instead is a mixture of pres-entation, media material, explanation, questioning, assignments, and dis-cussion that presume that the internal form of the knowledge will come together at some future time.

Indeed knowledge continues to evolve. Aside from the review time immediately before a major exam, however, there may be no point when it's presumed to be mastered, when the jigsaw picture is finally revealed. And if learning becomes comprehensive only a day before the final, it's sapped of significance by being scheduled, prepared for with review questions, crammed for, formed for the test, expressed on the test, and then dismissed.

Standard instruction wastes class time. For the sake of the argument, let's say you agree that the learning cycle comprises mainly your input and students' output. Let's say that you want to arrange for students to practice their knowledge. You agree with the necessity of effort and that they learn best by explaining what they know.

Once you have acknowledged they need both input and output, the next question is, "How much of each?" How much time for you and for them, you in the input phase and they in output?

You can answer with your own objective data if you'd like to explore a little. You might start by noticing when you begin and end an effort to explain, an activity distinctly yours. Then do as much of that as you can—fill the whole period with it—and allow them no other activity.

Under those conditions, plot their scores on tests and assignments as a baseline.

You can predict what will happen. As you talk on and on, their minds will shut off, erasing what you just said in order to listen to what you're saying now. You'll find diminishing returns as they don't talk and you talk too much.

Then gradually shift the proportions of the two activities—your effort compared to theirs. Back off the amount of yours, increase theirs, and watch what happens. You may "cover" less material, but by their questions, contributions, and comments, they'll absorb more of it and will reflexively dismiss fewer chunks of your presentations.

As you notice that they learn more as they talk more, aim to discover (1) how little you can say (2) that maximizes how much they can say (3) that increases their learning. As you change these proportions, I think you'll discover four decisive conditions. I would appreciate it if you let me know the data you collect. I estimate:

- You prepare and deliver a well-organized ten- to fifteen-minute presentation of new material.
- You synthesize it in question-and-answer form.
- You help them develop a complete hard copy of it by notes or handouts.
- You arrange for them to use forty-five minutes a period in practice explaining everything to a partner, back to the beginning of the term.

These conditions should come close to delivering the most new knowledge they can assimilate at the same pace it arrives.

THE POWER OF ACCUMULATION

That pace alone can yield enormous learning. Let's say every hour you get across a couple of ideas that way. As a ballpark figure, I think you could do that averaging five new ideas per class period without breaking a sweat (a piece with five parts, a process with five steps, an idea with five qualities, a couple of definitions containing a total of five notes of meaning, or a concept containing five features).

These are points substantial enough that each would be marked off as a separate error if missed on a test. You'd do your part with a quarter of the time, and students practice them for forty-five minutes as you direct.

Five points per class hour add up quickly. In 180 days, students accumulate 900 points of knowledge, 900 of the cellular units of learning for the year. With that accomplishment, would they feel competent and you pleased at their effort? If you and your fellow teachers did this for five instructional hours a day, together you'd leave students with 4,500 points of knowledge for the year.

Standard instruction fails to use the practice element.

Such a goal is achievable, I believe, only if teachers understand the role of practice. I refer to it here as *the repeated outward expression of an inward model to master it.* In general, we can agree that there's a direct correlation between practice of any skill, including knowledge, and its improvement: *The more I practice, the better I get.* Teachers practice their knowledge hourly as they express it, but usually *at* students. Their talk mainly exposes student minds to input.

Students begin practice only *after* the model of knowledge has been delivered and the arrow of action reverses. From ideas incoming, students turn to expression outgoing, but with four or five times as much expression of ideas as receiving them. If "your" time is the first ten to fifteen minutes for the input phase, the remainder is "theirs" for the practice phase. You deliver or arrange for the first understanding of new material, and in their time they master it.

In sports and music and all physical skills, the action is generally clear—performing the outward act. Parallel to this, learning has its own form of output—explaining. A model is presented to the mind, the mind grasps it at least in part, and practice occurs as the model is expressed in talking, discussing, writing, or drawing.

This outward expression of an idea once absorbed is what I term "the practice element." To the degree that it's employed in classroom activity, it deepens learning. Let's look at the customary ways people spend class time and try to identify the proportion of the practice element:

Teacher explains = zero practice element
Students ask questions of the teacher = minimal practice element
Teacher assigns written questions = minimal practice element
Teacher asks scattered questions = medium practice element
Students write out their knowledge = medium to high practice element
Teacher gives pop quiz = high practice element
Students do question-and-answer practice with partner = high practice element
Students perform their learning = high practice element
Students run all their learning as mental movie = high practice element

DRAWING ON THE PRACTICE ELEMENT

Let's understand each of these points:

1. Teacher explaining offers zero practice element. This is particularly important since teachers probably do 60 to 80 percent of the talk in most classrooms. Student minds readily go into triage, dismissing what the

teacher has already said because they are required to listen to what he or she is saying now. From a lengthy teacher presentation students may retain nothing.

Whoever talks is the one exerting output effort, the one practicing the knowledge, which is why teachers "learn a subject by teaching it." They do the input–output cycle over and over, with the proportion of output gradually increasing.

But if classroom talk averages 70 percent by the teacher, this leaves 30 percent for the students—in a class of fifteen to thirty, allowing a half minute to one minute talking time for each if talk occupies the entire period. In most classrooms, however, a few do most of the talking, and most of their comments are short enough to go on a Twitter message.

Teacher talk is important because it's often the most efficient way to transmit new material. But once the model is delivered, more teacher talk displaces student time practicing their learning to mastery. The model of the knowledge delivered remains on the surface.

2. Students asking questions of the teacher offers minimal practice element. While the activity itself may contain a medium practice element in which a student calls into awareness facets of the subject and expresses them at least partly, this occurs rarely enough that its influence can be discounted as a significant way to deepen learning for all. It helps mainly to clarify the model the teacher presented and thus draws on information currently available in the classroom.

3. Teacher assigns questions that students answer in writing by consulting the Internet, textbook, or handout. Since they typically just transfer knowledge from one spot to another, they may draw little on their own retained knowledge, giving this activity a minimal practice element. They can "look up" anything, cut and paste, and also track ideas organized on a basis other than their own thought structure. Often they just plug in unassimilated facts. While search-and-collect helps them form knowledge, no outward expression of their own inward model is involved.

4. Teacher asking scattered questions of students offers medium practice element. Often the questions follow closely on the presentation, so little depth of retention is presumed. Even deferring questions to the next day helps. But time allows only a few students to answer on selected points, leaving the rest coasting with the bulk of the learning so that benefit from answering a question isn't spread evenly among all students nor all ideas.

5. Students write summaries, essays, notes, and syntheses of their learning. This has a medium to high practice element. Thorough note taking during a presentation calls both on understanding what's presented and processing it quickly into a summary form—potentially at least a medium practice element.

The best practice arises from students writing while drawing just on what they've already learned from all their sources. As the assignment asks less of them, they depend more on stringing together what they collect, and the practice element diminishes. Because this tool can be used steadily with much learning, it's an important option.

6. Teacher gives a pop quiz. The form of the expression is confined to the design of the questions, but at least the quiz extracts outward expression of prior learning so that practice is involved. Its value is minimized, however, when it's used to assess students rather than help them deepen their knowledge, though it aids with that. Because it draws on and challenges students' depth of knowledge, we assign it a high practice element, although perhaps of limited use because employed infrequently.

7. Teacher breaks information into questions and answers and asks students to explain them to a partner until both know them. Here finally is clear-cut input and output. Presentation has occurred and knowledge has been gathered. The teacher has made the information understandable, expressed it in a practice-able form, and students explain it to each other. Students develop a mental model and then express it to deepen and expand it.

Such practice also has a logical end point that helps keep effort efficient: "You're done when you can explain it back anytime without looking." This activity has a high practice element and is especially valuable since it can occupy as much time as the teacher allows, works with both new and familiar material, and deepens knowledge probably more than any other activity.

8. Teacher uses knowledge learned in the prior activity for a daily or frequent performance of learning. A student name and a question are drawn randomly, and the student stands and answers impromptu. This activity cashes in on the value students place on peers' opinions and admiration and adds zest and interest to their learning. It has a high practice element, works with knowledge at all levels of sophistication, lends significant stimulation for little time spent, and helps motivate the partner practice above.

9. Teacher conducts mental movie, when students close their eyes and review the day's learning minute by minute for a high practice element. Students "run the film" of their day, bringing to mind everything they can recall. They discover the power of their mind to record with increasing detail everything they experience.

Teachers need not worry that children will waste time with their eyes closed. Children love to exert effort in socially valued ways, and this one matters because it expands their ability to practice and perform their knowledge in front of peers. It helps especially with subjects that build on visual structures such as math and science. Observable forms, relationships, and sequences are absorbed as imagination draws on them.

The more time teachers can spend in medium and high practice element activities, the better they promote learning in depth, the harder students work, and the easier the teacher's responsibility becomes. If we cease extinguishing knowledge, understand the power of steady accumulation, and use time and practice properly, learning is likely to take off.

SUMMARY

1. The U.S. system extinguishes learning.
2. Few teachers are adamant that students retain their material.
3. Engage students in the intent to retain knowledge permanently.
4. Engage them in preparing a comprehensive and complete hard copy of their learning.
5. Learning grasped perfectly is only at the beginning of its deepening.
6. Much instruction wastes time by miscalculating the proportion between input and output.
7. Enormous learning is accumulated if only the work of each hour isn't forgotten.
8. Standard instruction fails to fill class time with activities containing the highest practice element.

FIFTEEN

Seven Steps to Turn a Class Around: Key Levers for a Distracted Class

Your students show they could use a turnaround as they're distracted, marginally compliant, and exhibit a spectrum of effort and achievement. The prior chapters suggest seven steps a teacher can implement that alter their cooperation and raise their learning in a few days.

AN ICEBREAKER

First, your students could use an "aha moment" that restores their hope and offers a rationale for the changes you want to make. I picture you in front of a middle or high school class you have for only an hour a day. For three days, use the Study and Share activity.

If they'll cooperate with partners you assign, designate pairs ahead (see discussion of the bracelet aid in chapter 7). If they're cliquish, let them start off with whomever they wish. For subject matter, it may maximize interest to let them to choose any content they want, but with more focused students, you might have them open a new section of their subject or let them personally pick any section they haven't studied yet. Explain the format, adapting your vocabulary to their level:

> To learn something, we need both to receive it, such as by reading, and express it, such as by explaining it to someone. Today we'll do it this way: First, you spend ten minutes reading or studying something (specify the content you want them to address). I'll let you know when the time is up.
>
> Then for up to another five minutes each, you and your partner explain to the other what you each just read. Teach your partner what

135

you found out. When you both have said all you can, you can start the next round right away.

Find another partner, read another ten minutes, and explain to your partner what you read. In rounds after the first, you can also tell your partner what you learned before both from what you read and what your partner told you.

This is likely to be a high-energy experience. If you have two or three hours available or have an elementary class, you might expand the reading time to fifteen to twenty minutes, and sharing time increased as needed. On later rounds, continue to reassign partners and encourage them to share with their new partner also what they gathered in prior rounds or days.

From this activity, students will realize that if they just express their learning soon after it goes in and do that from time to time, they understand it better, make it socially relevant, and remember it. Implementing the following steps, you provide a more defined channel for their energy:

SEVEN STEPS

1. Measure Distraction Time Exactly and Deduct It from Free Time

The initial need is for better attention to your requests, so you first corral their focus. We can't obtain willing cooperation by repression, so we seek to engage them without arousing opposition or sabotage. Our leverage lies in a small thing that nonetheless matters to everyone—their free time.

Time *to the second* how long students spend not complying with direction, time waiting for them to quiet down. Add up their day's accumulation and deduct it from time spent at desired activities such as lunch, recess, sports, free time, release at the end of the day, and use of special equipment. This gives them an immediate reason to encourage each other to comply, bringing order to distractions, minimizing their interruptions, and shortening the transition time between activities.

I presume here that you're able to do this while maintaining a positive attitude. The context of this step must be that you *apply the consequence regretfully and sympathetically.* They should perceive your emotions as *for* them instead of *against* them. If you are harsh, irritated, or threatening, you can easily awaken in them a desire to compete with you and sabotage your effort. You want them regarding you instead as helping them learn something they'll use for a lifetime—to understand what's needed in situations they face and do the constructive thing.

2. Allow Students to Accumulate Bonus Time and Link It to Distraction Time

Since we want to encourage them as well as sanction misbehavior, we provide them a small benefit when they do give good attention to learning. As in the prior step, we measure distraction time but deduct it from *a presumptive bonus time* of, for example, five minutes for every hour of diligent attention to learning. As their bonus time accumulates, let them earn more freedom, recess, privileges, or special experiences.

3. Provide Appreciation Time Daily

Every day go around the class asking each student, "Who was friendly to you today and what did they do to show it?" or "Who gave you a good feeling today?"[35] This helps them reduce antisocial behavior, see each other as sources of pleasure rather than threat, and think in terms of good feelings.

Older students might explore the sources of good feelings with class discussions about the meaning of friendship, how they act differently when they want to make friends, how they themselves wish to be treated, and things they can thank each other for. The key is that in some way they recognize and acknowledge others' attempts to act positively toward them.

4. Practice Learning to Master It

Extract from every lesson the question(s) and answer(s) contained in it and save them. Assuming that a high stakes test included a question about everything you treat, what would it be?

Key points are best (1) written out in students' own summary notes so students use their own words to collect their understanding in one place and (2) practiced with a peer who asks the question and checks their answer against the correct one in their notes. With these two activities, students are more likely to master and claim their knowledge.

5. Perform Mastered Learning Every Day

The emotional reward that matters most to students comes from others' positive response to their effort. We can arrange for them to admire each other with a brief performance of learning hourly or at day's end: (1) Draw a question they've mastered; (2) draw a student's name; (3) have the student stand and give the answer; and (4) everyone applauds. They show off what they know. Content becomes more varied as students fill an individual bag with question slips that include their personal interests.

6. Score and Chart Mastered Learning

Students love to see scoreboards that faithfully report the results of their effort. They enjoy applying effort and claiming increments of improvement. Have a comprehensive chart on which they can record their growing number of mastered points of knowledge for all their subjects, all the questions they know the answers to, counted only once and maintained thereafter. A glance at this chart shows the amount of learning they claim to know "without looking or guessing."

7. Score Communication Skills and Other Behaviors You Want Students to Develop

The same pleasure at monitoring personal progress noted above can be applied to any ability such as communication skills from basic to refined. Invite them to tally their personal use of the skills and other positive behaviors (e.g., sharing, taking turns, cleaning up, obtaining supplies, helping another, doing a service unasked, and redirecting others' attention). Ask them to reinforce others' use of positive skills by tallying them as well. Students can change rapidly when they practice new skills and teachers and peers recognize their effort.

SYNERGISM OF THE STEPS

Each of the steps above supports success independently, but used together they're synergistic, gathering energy otherwise lost and channeling it into certifiable mastery. Several are rooted in students' social nature. They're touched by the opinions of those about them, cluster with others like them, do what brings others' explicit approval, and are rewarded by others' admiration for their competence.

As we channel such energy into learning, students realize that their effort gets results regardless of whether or not they quite felt like it that day. Applying effort to master one small chunk after another, they initiate an unbroken chain of successes and end the hour pleased at what they have done.

A way to appreciate this is to imagine yourself at a seminar. The instructor explains a new idea, you form an impression of it, and the instructor unexpectedly singles you out, asking you to stand and comment. You're immediately self-conscious as you stumble to your feet. Your words are necessarily sketchy, perhaps incompletely organized and inadequately thought through. Even as an educated professional, you may feel embarrassed even though your feeling is only a construct of the situation you're placed in.

We often set children up for just such embarrassment. Much seat-work and reading results in poorly formed knowledge. Fill in a blank or complete a sentence or answer a question at the end of a chapter, and what remains to demonstrate? The demonstration often depends on what the teacher provides instead of lodging in the student's own mental field.

For students to claim learning by the end of a lesson, they need a way to practice it right there so you identify the core point you want everyone to master and organize it concisely enough for them to do so. A teacher of a health class presents eight signs of cancer on a handout for all to master that period, and they do so with pleasure using (1) a hard copy of the idea, or a handout, text, or written notes; (2) a question that elicits it as an answer; and then (3) time to practice it with a partner until learned thoroughly.

Working with successive practice partners generates a sense of team-work, a feeling that "We're all in this together." Students develop conver-sation contracts. If Bill and Joe, who don't usually associate, practice math questions together, later they're more likely to accept each other and perhaps even talk about math. They want the competence but are driven more by the social reciprocity of gaining it.

DISPLAY OF COMPETENCE

Once students know the material, performing it energizes it further. You've identified everything you want retained during a given week and placed in a bag a slip for each question. You announce,

> Friday, we're going to have a stand-up performance. I'll draw a ques-tion, wait a minute while you think, and then draw someone's name. You leap to your feet, explain the answer, everyone applauds, and you sit down. We'll work our way through the questions we've learned this week.

Intense feelings can arise. Recall from your own schooling how keyed up you were when you had to prepare a report to the class. A teacher noted that most students he knew "would rather have a sharp stick in the eye" than stand up and talk. If he was right, we can do something about it. Whatever we want them to present to the class, we first have them prac-tice one-to-one quietly and safely until they're confident.

Once they're competent with knowledge, demonstrating it is a life-time satisfaction. Tasting it, they'll want to do it even better, so we set up performances of learning to ensure triumph. If we don't arrange the early steps, we don't get the later accomplishment. Without competence first, students don't enjoy expressing it later.

Personal display of competence is a powerful reason for effort just as an upcoming event in a sport shadows them as they practice. When they finally sit down, the crackle of applause conveys a *zing* of significance. Both preparing for and doing the performance *feel* important, making it a potential validator of competence for your entire curriculum. This picture of motivation applies early and at every step thereafter.

THE ISOLATED STUDENT

Of particular concern is the isolated student beyond the primary grades. His academic work is okay, but from early discomfort with peers he's decided to keep to himself, associate with others like him, or express his needs disruptively. How do you help him?

A valid basis for self-esteem is a history of successes. A child restores her confidence by looking back and remembering that she did valued things before. With some, the message was stunted, and the student concludes that success is hollow, that *working* didn't end up in good feelings. She does the tasks, but no bell rings nor applause erupts telling her, "This matters in your social world." We want her concluding, "I not only succeeded, *but what I did connected me to everyone.*"

We achieve this by drawing on academic competence in a way that solidifies peer relationships:

1. In partner practice, students bring to mastery everything learned till then. Pairing them successively with every other student enhances their acceptance into their group. It provides them a history with each other, expanding their social self-image to include the belief that they can get along with and work with anybody.
2. Stand-up performance of the bits and pieces of learning as question and answer draws out the isolated student and lets him know that he can face others' scrutiny. The performance of material practiced to the point of competence takes its place in his history of successes.
3. Applause by peers delivers the message, "You *matter.*" The unconscious is conditioned to hear, "People like what I did."
4. Keeping score of the success affirms the link between effort and results. Scores are stated to represent effort objectively and reliably, which helps students direct their effort to the results they want.

SUMMARY

1. As an icebreaker, use study and share, in which students read and then share with a partner.
2. Measure distraction time and deduct it from free time.

3. Apply consequences regretfully and sympathetically.
4. Allow students to accumulate bonus time and link it to distraction time.
5. Do appreciation time daily—acknowledging others who gave them good feelings.
6. Practice all learning in pairs to master it.
7. Daily perform mastered learning.
8. Score and chart mastered learning.
9. Score communication skills and other desired behaviors.
10. These steps together gather and channel energy otherwise lost.
11. Help the isolated student by developing competence others admire.

Notes

1. Steven A. Peterson, "There's no magic bullet to improve education," *Patriot-News*, Op-Ed, May 31, 2011.
2. The Critical Path Method (CPM) and Program Evaluation and Review Technique (PERT) are summarized succinctly at http://www.netmba.com/operations/project/pert.
3. For a more scholarly, detailed treatment of many issues touched on here, see Daniel T. Willingham, *Cognition: The Thinking Animal* (3rd edition), Prentice-Hall, New York, 2006, 600 pages; and by the same author, *Why Don't Students Like School: A Cognitive Scientist Answers Questions about How the Mind Works and What It Means for the Classroom*, Jossey-Bass, San Francisco, 2009. Willingham is professor of psychology at the University of Virginia. His website, www.danielwillingham.com, contains many excellent summary articles and blogs that expand understanding of key issues such as memory and practice.
4. Ronald S. Thomas, "My Nine 'Truths' of Data Analysis," *Education Week*, June 15, 2011. This thoughtful article deserves posting on the wall of education planners at all levels. It proposes that what students know is the point rather than how they score; that improving instruction is the aim, achieved through teachers closely allied in collaboration, reflection, and dialog; that data should identify weaknesses to correct and strengths to build on; that teachers must act differently; and that they need a strong rationale for the effort involved in gathering and interpreting data. In keeping with such guidelines, I propose here numerous ways to gather and present data that are motivating to students and tied directly to increasing their knowledge.
5. Jacob Bronowski, *The Ascent of Man,* British Broadcasting Corporation, London, 1976.
6. John Dewey, *Democracy and Education,* The Free Press, New York, 1916, page 36. The text is available online.
7. Ivan Pavlov, "Letter to the Young Scientists of Russia," *Science,* April 17, 1939.
8. When I was young, my father's business magazines turned up many basic truths about life. One that applies here is "strenuous limitation" as a fundamental quality of human achievement, analogous to a mill race. Water accomplishes a purpose only if it is

boundaried in a way that enhances its flow. Energy within those boundaries is what does the work. Here we ask for the design of a mill race through which children's effort, learning, and development can flow without hindrance.

9. With the drive of modern science to learn more and more about less and less, what's known now about working memory stands as one of the clearest evidence-based refutations of current pedagogy. We use working memory in quarter-second snapshots that come and go "hundreds of thousands of times a day" (University of California–Davis, "Working Memory Has Limited 'Slots'," *Science-Daily*, April 7, 2008. Retrieved June 25, 2011, from http://www.sciencedaily.com/releases/2008/04/080402212855.htm). The brain can sustain only three or four independent data slots at a time, but the quantity of information in them changes as the brain chunks up to work with groups of data (University of Missouri–Columbia, "Psychologists Demonstrate Simplicity of Working Memory," *ScienceDaily*, April 24, 2008. Retrieved June 25, 2011, from http://www.sciencedaily.com/releases/2008/04/080423171519.htm). Their ineffective use of working memory may be a significant factor in children's underachievement, but this deficit can be addressed: "The researchers believe this early assessment of children will enable teachers to adopt new approaches to teaching, thus helping to address the problem of under-achievement in schools. Without appropriate intervention, poor working memory in children, which is thought to be genetic, can affect long-term academic success into adulthood and prevent children from achieving their potential, say the academics" (Durham University, "Children's Under-achievement Could Be Down to Poor Working Memory," *ScienceDaily*, February 29, 2008. Retrieved June 25, 2011, from http://www.sciencedaily.com/releases/2008/02/080227205111.htm). Once information is processed in working memory, it may go into either fluid or crystalline intelligence. The former is important for many kinds of advanced problem solving while the latter is confined to a particular subject (University of Michigan, "Brain-training to Improve Memory Boosts Fluid Intelligence," *ScienceDaily*, May 6, 2008. Retrieved June 25, 2011, from http://www.sciencedaily.com/releases/2008/05/080505075642.htm).

10. Tim Beardsley, "Teaching Real Science," *Scientific American,* October 1992.

11. Saville Sax and Sandra Hollander, *Reality Games,* Warner Books, New York, 1972. The book contains a rich array of options for classroom use.

12. Richard P. Feynman and Ralph Leighton, *Surely You're Joking, Mr. Feynman: Adventures of a Curious Character,* W. W. Norton, New York, 1985.

13. The Harvard professor turned out to be Michael J. Sandel. His stimulating lectures about the moral basis of legal issues have attracted wide attention in Asia. In his article "Justice Goes Global" (*New York Times*, June 14, 2011), Thomas L. Friedman described Sandel's recent Asian tour as receiving rock-star-level acclaim, a clue to the priorities that emerging economies regard as significant.

14. A summary of Einstein's drill for overcoming distraction is available at http://www.concentrationexercises.com/concentration-exercises/albert-einsteins-distraction-index-drill-5.

15. Jacob Bronowski, *The Origins of Knowledge and Imagination*, Yale University Press, New Haven, 1978, page 105. This series of lectures offers insight into how the mind invents understanding from metaphor, imagination, and incoming data and develops conscious thought. A perspective possibly useful to educators is how the mind constantly draws on imagination to create an ongoing metaphor of experience. The activity of knowing is more fraught with nuance than our systematized education tends to recognize.

16. John Medina, *Brain Rules: 12 Principles for Surviving and Thriving at Work, Home, and School*, Pear Press, Seattle, 2009. The effectiveness of distributed versus massed practice has long been recognized in general, but the needs of the brain at certain stages call for thoughtful insight.

17. For plans for a learning contest raffle at different grade levels, contact the author. A contest and drawing can be simple and brief or cover the entire year curriculum with an extensive array of prizes. In a properly designed raffle, a few dollars allotted to cash prizes can motivate students to work harder. My experience suggests that the salary of a single teacher aide offered in cash prizes could transform learning in a district.

18. For decades people have changed their lives through the advice of Dale Carnegie in *How to Win Friends and Influence People*. A central theme is to take a genuine interest in others. Doing so guides behavior parallel to the first rule explained below. The first question in this category is a single brief sentence with four important words. Disucss each word separately with your class; for instance, "What does it mean to 'want'?"

19. The following points about communicating are also arranged for individual and group practice in self-rating in the Communication Skills Check Sheet located in the appendix of *A Compendium of Methods: Practice Makes Permanent*.

20. Richard J. Maybury, *Whatever Happened to Justice?* Bluestocking Press, Placerville, 1993.

21. These points about personal goal setting, titled Progress Ladder, are arranged as a check sheet for self-study in the appendix of *A Compendium of Methods: Practice Makes Permanent*.

22. These two life goals are suggested by Lester Levenson's *Release Technique*.

23. John Seeley, "The Forest Hill Village Human Relations Classes," John Seeley, *Personnel and Guidance Journal,* vol. 37, no. 6. February 1959. To look in on a current approach to the same principle, see Julia Steiny, "Julia Steiny: Weekly Circles Help Kids Get Closer to Adults and to Each Other," *EducationViews.org,* July 6, 2011.

24. Malina Saval, *The Secret Lives of Boys: Inside the Raw Emotional World of Male Teens,* Basic Books, New York, 2009.

25. James J. Heckman, Seong Hyeok Moon, Rodrigo Pinto, Adam Yavitz, and Peter Savelyev, *A New Cost-Benefit and Rate of Return Analysis for the Perry Preschool Program: A Summary,* National Bureau of Economic Research, Working Paper 16180, July 2010. This study summarizes the rigorous economic analysis establishing the critical importance of preschool experience for lifetime well-being and success. For a more user-friendly overview, see Alex Blumberg, "Preschool: The Best Job-Training Program," *National Public Radio,* August 12, 2011.

26. See note 20.

27. Gareth Cook, "Self-control in Childhood Predicts Future Success," *Boston Globe,* June 12, 2011. Cook summarizes the famous marshmallow experiment that separated children into those who couldn't resist the impulse to eat a handy marshmallow compared to those who could. Longitudinal study of these two groups has added much new information about the key role of self-discipline for all types of success in later life. There may be no single change in attitude we can teach that is more valuable to children's lives than an increase in self-discipline.

28. While Richard Bandler and John Grinder pioneered the understanding of rapport, Anthony Robbins provides an excellent explanation of it in *Unlimited Power,* Fawcett Columbine, New York, 1986, chapter 13. "The Magic of Rapport," page 230 ff.

29. Harvey Jackins, *The Human Side of Human Beings: The Theory of Re-Evaluation Counseling,* Rational Island Publishers, Seattle, 1965. This small book, illustrated with clear diagrams, is an easily understood explanation of how stresses shut down natural intelligence, how this process manifests, and how the body's built-in mechanisms attempt to free it. It provides a useful angle on much of what teachers find problematic, but standing as it does outside mainstream psychotherapy, has not received its due respect. Its value is better demonstrated by being translated into twenty-six languages.

30. Carlos Castaneda, *The Fire from Within,* Pocket Books, New York, 1984, chapter 2, "Petty Tyrants."

31. An interesting way to test this idea is gradually to increase the number of objects sustained simultaneously in awareness. Seated

comfortably, look at a feature of on the opposite wall, sustain that, and add second and third objects toward the left and right margins of the visual field. Holding those, add awareness of one's left shoe, the chair under oneself, and one's right arm on the table. Sustain all six. Add awareness of any continuing sound in the background such as the hum of a machine, and also provide a smell such as incense. Holding seven or eight items in steady awareness is extraordinarily difficult, but attempting to do this for a few minutes is also calming. I've used it to help people break severe headaches. Teach students how to do it in order to calm and focus their mind.

32. See *A Compendium of Methods: Practice Makes Permanent*, Section 51, "Academic Mastery Report," for a model.

33. The pilot program is explained in detail in *A Compendium of Methods: Practice Makes Permanent*, chapter 9.

34. David Ginsburg, "Quest for the Best Questioning Strategy: Cold Calling vs. Hand Raising," *Education Week* (online), June 10, 2011. Ginsburg offers a strong rationale for "cold calling" (random teacher selection of student) in place of hand raising as the better way to elicit comments and answers. His ideas expand the picture presented here.

35. I examine the rationale for and features of this experience in detail in *Changing Attitudes and Behavior: Practice Makes Permanent.*

Index

accumulation: of bonus time, 137; five ideas per hour, 130; gradual *a* of knowledge, 14; power of, 130–131

assignments: discarding, 20; individualized, 21; knowledge worth saving, 20; math building on prior, 20; moving knowledge around, 19–20; no expectation of mastery, 20; practice element low, high, 132–133; writing summaries of, 19

Bacon, Francis, 49

behavior: consequences for negative *b*, 111; following instructions, 105; reward positive, 110–111

behavioral knowledge, 57–69; behavior follows idea, 58; categories of modules, 61–69; change the idea, 58; checklist use, 57; driver's manual analogy, 58; frame as question and answer, 69; micromodules of, 60–61; plans for situations, 69; practice for perfect learning, 69; request specific actions, 59; school manual as checklist, 69; school manual needed, 59; score practice of, 60–61; thorough learning of, 60

biology: brain into triage, 22; depth missing from effort, 21–22; learn Latin names, 22; superficial learning of, 21, 47

black box, viii

Bronowski, Jacob, 3, 36

Castaneda, Carlos, 91

concentration, 31; units, 31, 32

communications. *See* perfect conversation

consequences: applied regretfully, 136, 141; from distraction time, 136

cookie principle, 22–23, 25; gain 900 min, 15 hrs, 37; and language learning, 23; repeating key action, 22. *See also* practice

curriculum: 50 categories, 36, 42; add more K–12, 42; incorporate all prior knowledge, 36; preserving curiosity, 37; targets of opportunity, 37

Dewey, John, 8. *See also* progressive education

Easy Learning, vii

education planning: basic mistake, 1; evidence-based, x; from direct experience, xi; guidelines for research, xi, 143; and hang glider, xi; laying aside frustrations, x–xi; redesign from solid idea, xi; theoretical validity, x

education reform: correlated with outcomes, vii; indirect causes, vii; struggle in, vii

effort, 15–25; admired for genuine *e*, 123; assessing effort, 15–16; assignments may lack, 25; centrality of, 23–24; conditions cause, quash, 17, 24; and cookie principle, 25; at dimensions of knowledge, 19; end-point to effort, 133; epiphany on, 17; essential for learning, 15; expand the focus, 18–19; focused thought, 2; gets results, 138; long-term retention from, 25; needed at different levels, 25; and poor learning of biology, 25; progress only by, 24; puzzled where to apply,

learn and lose system, 5–6, 125–127;
change intent, 127–128; extinguishes
learning, 14; redesign tests, 128;
steps to reverse, 127–128
learning: control can obstruct, 49. *See
also* experiential learning;
superficial learning
Lindh, Hillary, 30

mastery: criterion for, 127; definition
of, 13, 14. *See* permanence
Maybury, Richard, 81
meaning. *See* talking meaning
memory: ease of review, 51–52; end-
point of mastery, 52; few slots in
working *m* , 115; objective measure
of depth, 52; need for new
approaches, 144; recall deepens
retention, 52–53, 56; review vs
recall, 51–52; steps of perfect *r* ,
52–53; use with essential
knowledge, 53; working *m* discards
incoming, 37; working *m* misuse,
144
mental field, 43–50; about
relationships, 45; acquires
momentum, 45; basics before
advanced, 46–47; boy in poor
country, 48–49; can't be bought, 47;
clue to an education, 46;
conversation reveals, 50; definition
of, 50; develop by learn-save, 46;
enables advanced thought, 49;
fascination with, 45; fields compete,
44–46, 50; find satisfaction in, 44;
focus, grasp, express, 50; ideas
cohere, 43; independence from
external aids, 43; intent to think
differently, 47; just add more, 48–49;
lack of is apparent, 47; *mf* must
satisfy, 49; *mf* vs. desire for
efficiency, 47; open by
brainstorming, 47; reproduce
knowledge, 50; talk depends on, 50;
teacher asserts will, 44; will to
develop one, 45
mental movie, 54, 56; high practice
element, 133

misbehavior: from cognitive error, 18;
correcting, 17. *See also* behavior;
behavioral knowledge
modules for: anger, 64–65; becoming
independent, 67; borrowing, 61;
communicating, 66–67;
concentration, 65–66; connecting
thinking, 67; disagreements, 64;
energy, 64; friendships, 62–63;
goals, 67–69; good feelings, 63,
66–67; hurts, 64; inclusion, 66;
introducing self, 62; learning, 65–66;
listening, 66; perfect conversation,
66; power, use of, 67; progress
ladder, 67–68; self-control, 62;
sharing, 61; skill development, 65;
thanks, 61; trash, 62; understanding,
66

motivation: admired for effort, 123;
claim what enhances us, 34; and
conflicting messages, 127;
expectation spurs preparation, 123;
icebreaker, use of, 135; impossible
task, viii; instantly from conditions,
x; invest in, aspire to, 123; necessity
of intent, 126–127; notice others
positive acts, 17; parent listening,
49; raffle use, 145; sharing with a
peer, 49; what peers accept, 35;
unconscious cues, 121–122

partner practice: assign with bracelet
aid, 53, 56; bring all to mastery,
140–141; creates teamwork, 139;
high practice element, 133; of key
points, 137
Pavlov, Ivan, 11–12, 14
perfect conversation, 74–76, 77;
benefits of, 76; guidelines for, 74–75;
teaching *pc*, 76–77
performance, 117–123; admiration and
answering questions, 118;
admiration vs. attention, 118;
applause, effect of, 139; aspire to
achievable standards, 117; daily,
137; desire *p* efficiently, 141;
dignifying *p* with preparation, 119;
display of competence, 139; enlist

Note to the Reader

TO THE READER

If you find any of these ideas helpful in your classroom, you can assist us in passing them on to others by sharing a little information. Please open the website *howpracticemakespermanent.com.* There you will find four dialog boxes you can fill in:

1. What methods or ideas did you employ?
2. What results did they obtain?
3. How long did it take for results to show up?
4. Compared to preparing an average daily lesson, how difficult was the strategy you used?

Periodically I will summarize your comments and report them on the site, and also post other articles of interest. Many thanks for your help.

John Jensen

CPSIA information can be obtained at www.ICGtesting.com
Printed in the USA
BVOW010853140212

282857BV00001B/6/P